Who Stole The American Dream?

**The Book Your Boss
Doesn't Want You
To Read**

Burke Hedges

■ ■ ■

Books are available in quantity discounts.
For information, write:
International Network Training Institute (INTI)
6706 Benjamin Road, Suite 300
Tampa, Florida 33634
(813) 881-1638

Printed in the United States of America
January 1992
First Edition

ISBN 0-9632667-0-5

Published by INTI
Book Design by Sherrie A. Cuervo, *Design FX*

DEDICATION

This book is dedicated to my father,
Burke M. Hedges,
who passed away when I was a child.
And to the men and women who dare to take
advantage of our greatest right of all . . .
FREE ENTERPRISE!

CONTENTS

PHASE ONE: THE AMERICAN DREAM

PHASE TWO:
WHO STOLE THE
AMERICAN DREAM -- AND WHY

PHASE THREE:
WHY TRADITIONAL WAYS AREN'T
WORKING ANYMORE

PHASE FOUR:
THE TRUTH ABOUT NETWORK MARKETING

PHASE FIVE: NETWORK MARKETING AND YOU

ACKNOWLEDGEMENT

This book would never have been possible without the relentless support of John Fogg and Steve Price, two dear friends and business partners I admire enormously.

A special thanks to my wife Debbie and my two boys, Burkie and Nathen, for their continuing support in every endeavor I dare to undertake. To my mother, Maritza, and my step-father, Harley, for their faith in me. And to my partners, Tom Torti and John Tinari, for their tireless work.

A big "thank you" to all my teammates at NET International, Inc., for standing by me from the beginning: Liza West, Bob Henderson, Sherrie Cuervo, Sandee Lorenzen-Gray, Louise Knight, and the rest.

And finally, my gratitude and deep admiration to Ted von Schullick, a co-worker and good friend who passed away while this book was being written.

Why I Wrote This Book

Have you ever been made fun of . . . ridiculed . . . and abused . . . until finally, there came a time in your life when you said --

"ENOUGH IS ENOUGH!"

Well, I came to that point in my life. I'm mad as hell, and I'm not going to put up with it anymore!

So I'm writing this book to tell you the truth . . . to tell you what your real chances are today to make it in *conventional businesses* that are closing their doors every day -- and laying off people by the thousands!

I finally decided that someone needs to tell the truth about how the average person *could* succeed in an industry that is revolutionizing the way the world does business . . . how you could be your own boss and earn anywhere from part-time income to an absolute fortune in an unconventional business called Network Marketing.

Is Network Marketing a scam? . . . A scheme? . . . Or the American Dream? You deserve to know the truth. The whole truth. And nothing but the truth!

Read this book . . . and you be the judge!

■ ■ ■

Introduction

"America's Lost Dream"
Cover of *Newsweek*, March 2, 1992

Something was terribly wrong!

As I fit my key into the door lock, I had a strange, unsettling sensation. There was an almost electric tingling type feeling on the skin of my arms and hands. My stomach was suddenly empty . . . I felt oddly hollow and sick.

I opened the door and cautiously walked inside. It wasn't getting any better. It actually hurt now.

I looked around. I was in the right house. Nothing was out of place. It just didn't feel right – and the feeling was getting worse by the second.

Then I saw it. There was a hole right under the television where the VCR used to be. It was *gone!*

Oh no, I thought, what else did they steal?

Stop, Thief!

Somebody had broken into *my* home, messed around with *my* stuff, rifled through and ripped off *my* private things – and my wife Debbie's things, too. And my kids – they'd even stolen from my kids!

If this has ever happened to you, you'll probably never forget the feeling. I know I never will. As I remember this incident now, even though it happened years ago, those uncomfortable physical sensations return immediately.

It was awful – and it's *still* awful. I felt – dishonored . . . personally violated . . . angry. . . and absolutely powerless to do anything about it!

That's how we feel when someone steals from us.

And those are the feelings we have about someone breaking into our home and stealing stuff – just material things, which in my case, I went out and replaced in less than a week.

Imagine how much more shaken, angry and powerless we'd feel if someone stole so private and precious a thing as our *dreams*.

And that's just what they've done.

Somebody – or more accurately, a whole big bunch of somebodies – has stolen the American Dream. Right out from under our hard working noses.

We've had our hopes and dreams ripped off, our futures stolen and fenced by a bunch of freewheeling felons getting rich at our expense.

The American Dream Has Become a Myth

The American Dream is a fairy tale –
Not because it's not real. . .
Not because it's a thing of the past. . .
Not because it's not possible to achieve anymore,

either...

And *not* because we don't deserve it. Absolutely not that!

It's become a myth because the way we've been brought up – and the things we've been taught that we *had to do* to achieve the American Dream – simply don't work anymore.

And what's more, that whole business of "Get a college degree, work your way up the corporate ladder or start your own small business and achieve your dreams..." – could be a *setup*. For an increasing number of us, it's turned into a con, a scam and a scheme the big shot power people use to get us to work our lives away trading too much time for not enough money just to make *them* rich!

Just thinking about it brings up the same feelings in me that I had when my home was broken into . . .

With one exception. I don't feel powerless. Not anymore.

I found a way to get back The American Dream.

But before I tell you my way – the average person's way – let me ask you some questions.

What is the American Dream?

Is the American Dream going to college and getting a degree? Now, you know that works for some, but really – how many? And isn't it true that for the doctors, lawyers, and Indian chiefs of government and corporate America – the future isn't what it used to be? How many college grads find work in their chosen fields today? How many are doing that same work ten years later, or even five? Not very many.

Is the American Dream getting a good job? Working for a living? Can you get a job where you can earn what you're worth . . . where you'll get rich . . . and find fulfilment . . . and gain freedom . . . trading your time for money?

Did you know that over half of all first time heart attacks occur between the hours of 8 AM and 10 AM *Monday morning?* That tells me that people would rather die than go back to work!

There's no loyalty in corporate America anymore – and no security, either. According to Paul Zane Pilzer, a world renowned economist, we're headed for as much as 20 percent unemployment by the year 2000.

Is the American Dream owning your own small business? I did that. Made a million dollars – and it cost me $1.2 million to do it!

Did you know that 90 percent of all small businesses fail in the first year . . . and 80 percent of the survivors close their doors in the next five? And 80 percent of *those* never see year 10? Is owning your own *conventional* small business the way to achieve The American Dream?

Now notice, I said, *"conventional."*

The Times We Live In

We live in unconventional times, and they call for unconventional ways of doing things. New and better and different ways.

Ideas that used to take 50 years to be born, grow and mature – now take only five. Everything's changing – and changing so rapidly that the great success stories of just a few short years ago are outmoded, dying dinosaurs today.

Here's an example: vinyl records.

If you owned a successful business making records and albums in 1985, you were probably a very rich person – a millionaire many times over. Where would you be today – just a few years later? Cassette tapes and compact disks rule the roost today. Almost nobody buys records anymore.

Are you beginning to see the picture?

Ladies and Gentlemen, tomorrow is happening *today*. If you can't see it, if you don't know what's coming, you're going to be left behind. And not just one or two steps behind either – *miles* behind! And things are moving so fast you may *never* catch up – ever!

Look, if you're not already in place, at the top, on a leading edge career track where your job is out there literally working in the future today, you've got no better than one chance in ten thousand of making it to the top of anything else. Believe me, it's true. What's left over are the cheap, unfulfilling service jobs – cleaning up after or waiting on the hot shots who are where the action is.

Look around you. It's already happening.

The Changing American Workplace

Do you think "big steel" and U.S. heavy industries are going to make a comeback? Who's going to replace a robot or some other error-free, automated machine that just replaced 20 human beings for less than half the money they were being paid – *and* that does a better job? Try working in Detroit . . . Pittsburgh . . . West Virginia . . .

Let's face it, blue collar jobs are becoming extinct.

So, what about white collar jobs?

The answer to that is two words: First – *technology*. And second – *profits*.

Look, 35 percent of all white collar workers – we're talking millions and millions of people here – will be out of work, collecting unemployment ('til it runs out), sadly searching for the same kinds of jobs their former employers just eliminated completely in some other company that hasn't streamlined yet. How about the 70,000 people GM is laying off? Or the 40,000 people IBM let go? Where will they go for work? What will they do?

Good luck.

You must have seen the unemployment reports. Big corporations are laying off people by the tens of thousands – more than 700,000 in 1992! Why?

Changing times . . . those workers just aren't needed anymore – and who can afford them anyway?

Look, jobs are being cut left and right and those companies are now accomplishing the same work – or more work – with fewer people! The only thing climbing higher than unemployment is the stock market! The rich *are* getting richer – and the poor...? We all know the answer to that!

College, corporate careers, small business, blue collar, white collar. . . what's left?

What's left is a way of life and work called Network Marketing – the most powerful form of distribution of goods and services for the 1990s. A new and better way of working and living. A proven industry that people from every walk of life are turning to. A way for the average person to achieve the American Dream.

That's what this book is about.

You Deserve to Know the Truth About Network Marketing

Why?

Because it will be in your future in one of three ways:

• You'll be one of the people who's making it happen; or...

- You'll be one of the people who's watching it happen; or . . .

- You'll be one of the people wondering *"What happened?"*

You'll either be one of the millions of ordinary men and women who achieve extraordinary lifestyles through Network Marketing – or you'll be one of those who wish they had.

I guarantee you that in five to ten years, if you're not a Network Marketer, you'll be one of those other millions of people throughout North America and the world buying things from them . . . making things they buy. . . serving them or waiting on them.

Bold talk? Yes – the boldest. And yes, I've earned the right.

I had the American Dream stolen from me – just like I'm saying most of you have. I've experienced those feelings in the pit of my stomach: broke, scared, couldn't pay the bills, couldn't provide for my wife and kids, no vacation, no fun, no future – frustrated, angry and feeling powerless to change it.

Then, I discovered Network Marketing. And, yes – perhaps like you – I was skeptical at first. It sounded too good to be true. I felt it was just some sales scam – you know, a pyramid scheme.

But hey, it didn't cost me anything to check it out – and what if it was true? What if it really was my ticket to The American Dream? I couldn't afford to risk losing out!

They say the mind is like a parachute – it doesn't work unless it's open. So, I opened up my mind. I tucked my doubts and disbelief under my arm and took a look.

What I found was that Network Marketing really *was* simple – even I could do it! It was fun, too. There were lots of people to help me do it. I got to make a powerful, positive difference in hundreds, even thousands of people's lives. And, yes, I made money, too – a fortune, in fact!

But who cares what I did? Who cares what I think?

The Important Question Is: What Do *You* Think?

... Is Network Marketing right *for you*? Can you be successful in Network Marketing – *will* you?

I don't know the answer to that. But I do know that you absolutely, positively owe it to yourself to learn the truth about Network Marketing.

I mean – *what if ... ?*

What's it going to take for you to learn the truth, the whole truth and nothing but the truth? The cost of this book and a couple of hours of reading – max.

It will be time and money well and wonderfully spent. That's a promise.

You see, in my opinion, Network Marketing is the wave of the future.

In my opinion it's called "the people's franchise" for a good reason.

My opinion is that Network Marketing is putting the freedom *back* into free enterprise.

It's my opinion that Network Marketing is the very best way in the world – perhaps the *only* way – for average people like you and me to live far-above-average lives.

But that's *my* opinion.

In *Fathers and Sons,* the Russian author Ivan Turgenev wrote:

"I share no man's opinion. I have my own."

So, it's really *your* opinion of Network Marketing that counts – isn't it?

See, it doesn't really matter what my opinion is.

You've got to know for yourself.

What *really* matters is what *you* think and feel about Network Marketing. In short, you've got to know what's in it *for you!*

I promise you this: if you'll just take the time to learn about who stole The American Dream – and then determine for yourself if you can get it back with Network Marketing – then you'll know if Network Marketing is the right vehicle for you.

No Excuses

Now I know some of you will make excuses for not investigating this industry. Some people will say, "I don't have the time" ... or "It's not for me" ... or "I'm too old to try something new" ... and so on.

All these half-baked excuses remind me of a guy who wanted to mow his grass, but his mower was broken. So he went next door to his neighbor's house and asked if he could use their lawn mover.

"Sorry," said the neighbor. "I can't lend you my lawn mower because my wife is cooking beef stroganoff.

Startled by his neighbor's response, the man asked, "What does your wife cooking beef stroganoff have to do with you lending me your lawn mower?"

The neighbor looked him square in the eye and replied, "If I don't want to loan you my lawn mower, any excuse will do!"

How about you – are you accepting just any excuse to avoid finding out about this industry? Hey, if you've made all the money you'll ever spend (and you have the time and freedom to enjoy it)... you probably don't need to investigate the possibilities of becoming successful in Network Marketing.

But if you're like most of us, you've got everything to gain and nothing to lose by finding out the facts about this industry.

There's no better time to check it out than right now!

And if you decide that Network Marketing is for you, you'll look back on this moment in time as the single most important moment in your life!

This could be that special moment when you start to take control of your life again . . . the moment you begin to feel the freedom, security and happiness of The American Dream—the moment you start to make it your own.

■ ■ ■

Phase One:

The
American Dream

■

CHAPTER ONE

The Myth of The American Dream

What is The American Dream?

We all have our own unique version of what The American Dream means. Ask a million people to describe their dreams and you'll have a million separate, distinct and uniquely individual pictures. However, there are a number of things that all our dreams have in common, no matter how different each of us is.

We all want freedom and security for ourselves and our families. We want more money than we have now. We want health and happiness.

Basically, we want what we don't have.

Isn't that true for you?

The sad fact is, tens of millions of people aren't living their dreams at all, are they?

The Truth About the American Dream

Most of us aren't free to live where we choose – in the kind of house we want – because we simply can't afford it.

What else do we want? A top notch education for our kids . . . travel and vacations . . . entertainment... recreation . . . going out to dinner . . . new clothes . . . and a whole host of other possessions and possibilities for realizing our dreams.

So what happens? We finally get that special car that we want – and then stay home because we can't afford to go out! Unfortunately, we're forced to pick just one of the things we really want – and sacrifice everything else.

We've made settling for less a habit!

Today, people aren't free to do what they'd really love to do for a living – what they're really good at. They're strapped to a job they don't like – or worse, one they hate – because they just have to have that paycheck to survive.

I've done that – working for $5.50 an hour building boats for someone making a whole lot more money than me. Waiting on tables for $150 a week . . . *including* tips! Doing work I hated. Hanging out with my buddies after work. Going nowhere in a hurry.

That's when I asked myself, "Is that all there is?" I used to hear that song in my sleep!

It was the pits, yet I was too scared to leave and take a chance on something better. I knew I was worth more than $5.50 an hour. But I depended on that paycheck – and I had a family depending on me!

Sound familiar?

You know, the truth is only one half of one percent of the people in America make over $100,000 a year.

And that's just about how much it takes today to even get close to financial security.

The Bottom Line

The cornerstone of The American Dream has always been financial freedom – enough money to do *what* you want, *when* you want to do it.

That's not to say that money alone is what we desire most. We all know it's not the money, *but what the money will buy.* And it's true that one thing money does buy in a society like ours – is freedom.

Money builds churches and schools and puts clothes on our children's backs.

Another thing money can buy today is health.

The rising cost of medical care in the United States has made it virtually impossible for people of average means to afford even basic medicines and proper health care. By the year 2000, experts predict the cost of health care as a percentage of income will reach 20 percent – more than twice what it was in 1980!

What about adequate health insurance coverage? Who can afford it? (Much less the finances to deal with an unexpected emergency!) In 1990, nearly four out of every ten Americans in the U.S. had no health insurance at all! Well over 35 million people under 65 years of age – in the richest country in the world – have no way to take care of themselves or their families in the event of an accident or illness – *no way!*

And is there any greater cause of stress – which more and more physicians say is a primary contributor to sickness and disease – than anxiety and worry over money?

The shocking truth is that medical research proves the affluent are significantly healthier than the average American!

You bet money can buy health – and lots of it!

How about happiness? They say it's the one thing money *can't* buy.

We all know *that's* not true. Look at a child on Christmas morning.

Freedom, security, money, health and happiness. We were never meant to be forced to pick just one or two.

Paying the Price

Sir James Barrie, who wrote the classic fairy tale *Peter Pan*, once said:

"Dreams do come true . . . . You can have anything in life if you will sacrifice everything else for it."

Can you believe that?! Do we really have to give up everything else to get a little of what we want?

How much freedom do you have if you can't pay the mortgage or the rent?

What happiness is there if you don't have security . . . if you can't afford good health and medical care?

What good is having anything if you have to give up everything else to get it?

No, the *real* American Dream is to have it all.

But the sad truth is, the vast majority of North Americans today don't stand a chance of getting what they want out of life. For them, The American Dream has become a fairy tale. A myth.

For an alarming number of people, it may even have become The American Nightmare!

■ ■ ■

CHAPTER TWO

Why?

Walt Disney once said, "All our dreams can come true – if we have the courage to pursue them."

If what Uncle Walt said is true, then the only thing standing between people and their dreams is *"the courage to pursue them."*

Let's talk about that for a minute...

Was it a *lack of courage* that made us "put away the childish things" we dreamed of as kids? Was it *lack of courage* that forced us to give up the dreams and aspirations of becoming a ballerina – baseball star – doctor – actor – astronaut... and settle into something more *reasonable?*

Was it a *lack of courage* that sent high-schoolers into four years of college – at a cost of $40,000 or more – only to graduate and find there weren't any jobs for them. Or if they did find a job, it sure wasn't anything they studied in college... anything they'd spent years learning how to do... anything they really enjoyed doing.

Was it a *lack of courage* that got millions of blue collar men and women laid off as "dinosaur" industries died out . . . as business after business closed, as farms were bought up and advancing technology made tens of thousands of jobs obsolete?

Auto workers in Detroit, steel workers in Pittsburgh, coal miners in West Virginia, oil riggers in Houston, production workers in New England's defense companies, and hundreds and hundreds of small farmers throughout North America – do these people all simply *lack courage*?

Was it a *lack of courage* that makes hundreds of thousands of smart, committed, hard working white collar people loyally give "the company" all *the best years of their lives* – only to find their pay slashed. . . or suddenly threatened with layoffs . . .or actually flat-out fired?

What about the 1,700 people laid off at American Express . . . the 1,500 at Pepsico . . . the 13,900 at United Technologies . . . the 20,000-plus office workers, supervisors and middle managers at GM . . . the 40,000 employees at IBM . . . or all the folks at Eastern and Pan Am? How about the men and women in real estate, stock brokering, insurance, education, sales, auto dealerships, hotels, food service, etc. . . ? Did these people really all just *lack the courage* it takes to pursue their dreams?

Is it a *lack of courage* that's responsible for more than 20 percent of all office space in America lying empty and unused in the early 1990's?

Was it a *lack of courage* that forced countless strong, hard-working men and women to toil their entire working lives . . . only to be forced to retire before they were ready?

Really – is it the *lack* of *courage* that's missing? Is that why we don't have our dreams?

What About Your Dreams?

Are you living and working the way you thought you would—the way you wanted—the way you choose?

Do you have what you dreamed of as a child . . .?

What you went to college for . . .?

Were you rewarded by your company for your years of hard work and loyalty?

Will you able to retire like you want to? And after retirement, when you finally have the time . . . will you have the money to enjoy your life, your family and your friends?

According to Mr. Disney, if your dreams haven't come true, it's because you didn't have the *courage* to pursue them.

Is that really true?

Are we really all just a bunch of *cowards* . . .?

Nonsense!

I truly believe that each and every one of us has an inner fire, a basic survival instinct to fight back when the chips are down.

We're not cowards—not our friends, not our family, not our children.

I guarantee you, none of us lacks courage! What we need is a vehicle to help us get back our dreams.

So, What's Wrong?

I'll tell you what I think – we're frustrated. Fact is, we're more than frustrated—we're angry! And we feel powerless to change the way things are.

You and I may be mad as hell, but there sure doesn't seem to be much we can do about it – or can we?

Folks, The American Dream is not a myth. It's real– very real.

Don't you dare let anybody take your dreams away!

We're not cowards. We're victims of a crime. The

crime of the century. Somebody stole The American Dream.

And it's not so much The American Dream itself that they took from us because we both know the dream is still there – somewhere.

What they stole was our ability to get at it. What they stole was *our belief* that we can have it.

It's part of a cover-up that keeps telling us, "Do what everybody else is doing.... Don't rock the boat.... Hey, you could lose what little you've got now – don't blow it!... There is no other way."

No wonder that by age 65, ninety-five percent of all people are either dead, dead broke, still working ... or dependent upon family, church or state. Only five percent are financially independent!

I challenge you to quit doing what 95 percent of the people do – which is to end up at age 65 struggling to get by.

I'm going to show you how to be one of those five percent who own their own lives! I'm going to show you how you can have everything you've ever dreamed of having by becoming one of those special five-percenters!

■ ■ ■

Phase Two:

Who Stole the Dream
– and Why
■

CHAPTER THREE

Pyramid Schemes

You've probably heard some people call Network Marketing a "pyramid scheme."

Do you know what that means? The reason I ask is that most people have *no idea* what a pyramid scheme really is.

The truth is, a multi-level pyramid is a natural structure. *Every single organization in the world* that distributes goods and services of any kind is shaped like a pyramid, with multiple levels that get bigger as they go down.

Here's how noted author and educator Dr. Karl Dean Black explains it:

"Delegation creates a multi-level pyramid. Our government is a multi-level pyramid. So are our schools and churches. All successful businesses, because they distribute goods and services, end up shaped like a multi-level pyramid.

"In any multi-level structure, the power comes from the bottom. Our government distributes services down a pyramid, but we give it power from the bottom with our votes. Marketing companies distribute products down a pyramid, but we give them power from the bottom with our dollars. So pyramids set up a flow

that runs both ways: first down, then up. Value flows down the pyramid; power, in response, flows up. If value stops flowing down, power (in the form of dollars or votes) stops flowing up, and the system collapses."

So, according to Dr. Black, American business, government and education – are *all* pyramids.

Network Marketing is indeed a pyramid, just like IBM, General Motors, colleges and universities, the U.S. Government and your church.

So it's not the pyramid structure itself that makes something a *"pyramid scheme."* There's nothing wrong with the concept. It's what people do with it – how they use or abuse it.

Two Sides of the Pyramid Coin

I use a pretty bold analogy to make this point: sex.

On one side of the coin, sex is making love, two people uniting, becoming one, the passion and pleasure of creating new life together.

On the dark side, there is violation, rape and abuse.

It's not sex itself that's wrong or bad. It's the individual experience and expression of it that makes it either beautiful or ugly.

It's the same with a pyramid. There's nothing wrong with something having a pyramid structure. What makes something a pyramid "scheme" is when, as Dr. Black pointed out, " . . .*value stops flowing down.*

Now, this may surprise you, but there are two different kinds of pyramid schemes: illegal ones and *legal* ones.

Let's talk about them both.

■ ■ ■

CHAPTER FOUR

Illegal
Pyramid Schemes

An illegal pyramid scheme is a money-making scam where the people at the bottom put money in, but value doesn't flow down to them in response. It's the kind of thing where a few people at the top get rich, while the majority of people – the ones on the bottom – lose out.

Examples are chain letters and the "airplane game," a money-tree game which was popular a couple of years ago until the government shut it down.

How a Chain Letter Works

One day, you get a letter in the mail. You may or may not know the person who sent it to you. Usually the letter is filled with compelling, even inspiring language about prosperity . . . how you deserve to be rich, even how God meant you to be wealthy . . . and how, if you do the following simple steps, in two to four weeks, thousands to tens of thousands of dollars will appear in your mail box as if by magic.

Something for nothing. And here's all you have to do to get it.

Somewhere on the letter is a list of names and addresses. You take the name on the top of the list,

erase it, send that person the cash or money order –
$1, $5, $10, $100, whatever – and you add your name
to the bottom of the list. Make 10 to 100 copies of the
letters and send them to everybody you know.

There's usually a sense of urgency about all of this.
The letter may encourage you to send your money and
mail out your copies that same day, or within 48 hours
at the most. Some letters even include threats, such
as, "If you break the chain, you will be punished with
a plague of poverty – or someone will put peanut
butter in your VCR."

Seriously, some chain letters I've seen tell stories of
people who lost homes, businesses, *even died,* because
they broke the chain!

And "breaking the chain" is exactly the problem.

If everybody who received a chain letter responded
by sending money to the name on top of the list – and
if all those people also sent out their own copies of the
letter, and so on and so on – then everybody but the
people at the very bottom of the pyramid *would*
actually receive thousands of dollars in their mailbox.
But it never happens. It can't.

The people who start the chain letter, and the ones
near the top who "get in early" before it gets busted,
are the only ones who stand a *chance* of making money
– and everybody else loses.

The Illegal Lotteries

Any game of *chance* involving money is gambling,
and gambling is illegal unless it's under the vigilant
eyes of local, state and federal officials.

The U.S. Postal Service has an investigation/en-
forcement division whose main mission in life is to
catch people like chain letter participants, put them

in jail and throw away the key. These guys are relentless. They carry badges, handcuffs, guns, the whole bit. And since they are "the Feds," their power extends everywhere. IRS agents are pussy cats compared to these guys.

A chain letter is an illegal lottery. Outside of Tuesday night bingo at the local church or a non-profit group's fund-raising raffle, the state and federal governments are the only people who can operate a lottery legally.

Now, another variation on this get-rich-quick, money-tree scheme is the now-infamous "airplane game." Here's how it's played.

A bunch of people get together and form an imaginary "airplane." The plane has passengers, a co-pilot and a pilot. Passengers can buy a seat on the plane for $1500, $6000 or even as high as $50,000, depending on the particular game being played.

Once you become a passenger, you must go out and recruit new passengers to buy seats on the plane for the same amount of money you paid for your seat. Each time you bring on a new passenger, you move forward one seat towards the cockpit. When you bring on enough people, you become the co-pilot . . . and eventually the pilot.

Now, you bring your new passengers, with their cash in hand, to a once-a-week meeting. That's where they turn in their money and get a seat on the plane. That's also where you get "coached" on how to bring people into the game. The co-pilot and pilot are usually excellent coaches. You'll see why soon.

So, where does the money go? To the pilot. See, when you're the pilot, all those new passengers who came to the meeting give you their money right then and there. Ten new passengers, at $1500 each, is

$15,000 *cash*. In most airplane games, it takes four to six weeks for a new passenger to move from the back of the plane to the pilot's seat.

What does a pilot do then? Flies off into the sunset of success – or, buys a seat on a brand new airplane. And when you've done it twice, hey, move up to a $6000 per seat airplane game. $6000 times 10 is $60,000 – or $10,000 per week, if all goes right and the plane doesn't crash.

But it does. Airplanes crash when there aren't enough new passengers – that is, when the people on the plane run out of friends and family with $1500 to spend in hopes of hitting the pilot's jackpot. What happens then? The people who became pilots early on made a quick little fortune – and the rest of the folks are out $1500 each. Why? No value ... no product or service is being exchanged for money.

Very Few Winners – Lots of Losers

That's the second reason these money games are illegal – they rip people off.

Somebody – and eventually lots and lots of somebodies – will break the chain or fail to recruit more new people. When one person isn't able to get enough other people to send money and letters or play the game – he or she is out. You don't get your money back. That's the risk you take.

A few people at the top make a fortune and everyone else down at the bottom of the pyramid never gets a cent.

Some of these games (like the airplane game) require thousands of dollars of cash up front in order to play. There are lots of people out there who've lost lots *and lots* of money when the chain broke and the plane "crashed."

And one thing is true about every one of these pyramid schemes – sooner or later they *always* crash and burn.

In fact, when the State Attorney General of New York finally busted the airplane game, they discovered it had roots in organized crime. It was started by the Mafia!

Ponzi Schemes

There's one more category of illegal pyramid. It's called a "Ponzi scheme," named after an Italian immigrant, Carlo "Charles" Ponzi.

Ponzi came to America from Canada where he spent some time in jail for passing bad checks. He ended up rather quickly in Federal prison in the U.S. for smuggling illegal aliens into the country.

If Ponzi had been a botanist, history would be forced to recognize him as the man who discovered the "money tree."

Here's what he did.

At that time, the post offices of the world issued what were called International Reply Coupons, which in essence were certificates good for postage stamps throughout the world. Ponzi's idea was to purchase these coupons in countries where the inflation rate was high and redeem them in countries where the rate was low. Simply put, this enabled him to buy low and sell high.

On the strength of these coupons, Ponzi created the Securities Exchange Company and issued his own "promissory notes." An investor could purchase one of Ponzi's notes with a face value of say $150 for $100. In just 90 days, the investor could redeem the note for its full value. In the days when banks were regulated to offer four percent interest, Ponzi's notes promised an extraordinary return!

At first, Ponzi's investors were dubious and risked only $10 or $20. However, after earning 50 percent interest on their money a couple of times, they felt more secure and soon began to invest thousands. Ponzi also cut the time frame down to 45 days to sweeten the deal for investors. (It did!)

In no time at all, Ponzi's empire grew to staggering proportions. One million bucks would flow into his offices every day! As his investors got rich and spread the word, Ponzi got even richer. He was hailed as a financial genius. He now owned a local bank – the Hanover Trust Company – lived in the posh suburb of Lexington, Massachusetts, and was known far and wide as "The Great Ponzi."

Only one problem.

Ponzi's "money machine" operated by robbing from Peter to pay Paul. He took the money investors sent in today to pay the money due tomorrow on previous investors' notes. It was a merry-go-round of money that seemed to work perfectly. The International Reply Coupons that were supposed to be the source of Ponzi's wealth building investments didn't exist. Ponzi never purchased more than $100 worth of them.

And one day in 1920, the merry-go-round stopped dead.

A public relations man whom Ponzi had hired to handle the attacks from the Boston press took one look at what was actually going on – and blew the whistle.

Ponzi was convicted of mail fraud and sentenced to nine years in prison. He jumped bail, moved to Florida, sold swamp land in a real estate scam, got caught and was returned again to prison. Eventually, he was deported back to Italy. Ponzi died alone and broke in 1941.

Round and Round and Round...

The full amount of money lost in the Ponzi scheme will never be known. Over $15 million (in 1920 dollars) was paid out to "investors" before the "business" collapsed. Carlo "Charles" Ponzi was the proud father of one of the most incredible inventions of all time – the illegal pyramid scheme.

What made Ponzi's scam an illegal pyramid scheme was the merry-go-round principle. As long as money was coming in, money would continue to go out. Investors were paid in full, on time, and everyone was happy. However, when the money *stopped* coming in, the "jig was up." The same thing would have happened if the amount of money coming in had begun to slow down.

Eventually, the people who invested late in the game lost their money.

Some of them lost everything they had.

What Ponzi did was to live on the "float" – you know, like writing a check today to pay yesterday's bills based on money that won't arrive until tomorrow in the hope that the check won't be cashed until some time next week - and so on and so on.

Sound familiar? Probably too familiar.

You know, it seems to me that a whole big part of the world of government, education and business today is doing just what Carlo Ponzi did.

You be the judge.

■ ■ ■

CHAPTER FIVE

Legal
Pyramid Schemes

It should be obvious to you now why illegal pyramid schemes are against the law. Illegal gambling, illegal lotteries, outright rip-offs that permit a select few to get rich at the expense of many others... these acts break human laws—legal rules which were enacted to protect us against injustice and foul play.

But there's another set of laws that govern how humans live and work. Natural laws. God's laws. It's these laws that Dr. Dean Black was speaking about when he said that pyramids collapse when there's no value flowing down to balance the power of the dollars or votes flowing up.

The Biggest Pyramid Scheme in the World

The alarming truth is that there are many organizations and enterprises in the world that are without a doubt pyramid schemes of the highest (or more accurately, *lowest)* order. In fact, the biggest pyramid scheme in the entire world *is legal!*

It's run by the United States Government.

It's called Social Security.

There's not a person under 50 in America who should expect to collect all of his or her Social Security benefits at retirement. Everybody knows the Social Security Administration will be broke by the time it's their turn to collect. Really, what is Social Security but a huge pyramid scheme!

You pay a percentage of your earnings every month of your working life – and a pretty big chunk it is, too – so that one day, when you retire – at what, 62 years old? – you'll get a monthly benefit check 'til the day you die.

Now, the U.S. government gets all this money from everybody who works or earns money in America, and what do they do with it? They pay the people whose "investments" are due now, just like Carlo Ponzi. If there's any extra, they *gamble* with it. That's right – they "invest" in stocks and bonds ... they gamble with your future and try to make *more* money so that by the time it's your turn to get your payoff – there'll be enough to go around.

Right now, they're doing okay with this game, because between 1946 and the mid-1960s, 76 million kids were born into a huge mega-group of humanity called the Baby Boom. All these millions of boomers have been donating money into the fund all their working lives, and they're paying for those folks who are old enough to be getting social security benefits right now.

But what happens when it comes time for the first of those 76 million baby boomers to start collecting – which should occur in about 2010? You guessed it ... there won't be any money left!

After the baby boom came the baby bust. There have been nowhere near the same number of births since the baby boom – and probably never will be again. So, there will be far fewer people paying in money than there are taking it out. It's already happening. In business terms that's called a negative cash flow. Too much month at the end of the money!

What's going to happen when the first wave of baby boomers takes out so much money that there's nothing left? The crash of the airplane game will be like a fly going down the toilet compared to the nationwide devastation when Social Security crashes!

You tell me: Is value flowing down this pyramid?

Doesn't this sound a lot like Carlo Ponzi's scam?

How the Rich Get Richer

The essence of all pyramid schemes – the illegal ones *and* the legal ones – is that the guys at the top get rich while everybody else loses.

It's like when corporate CEOs get paid millions and millions in pay, perks and benefits . . . while the company and the stockholders lose money. All too often employees are forced to take pay cuts while they struggle to make ends meet – or worse yet, they get laid off.

American chief executives make around 100 times more than the guys on the factory floor. That means the wage-earning worker earns $30,000 annually while the boss makes $3 million! Compare that to economic powerhouse Japan, where CEOs' pay averages about 17 times what their employees earn.

If you're searching for a place to increase corporate profits in tough economic times – hitting CEOs' pay is the mother lode!

The big three auto makers in Detroit will lose – collectively – nearly $10 billion in 1991. What do you think Lee Iacocca got paid? In 1990, a year when profits fell 17 percent for Chrysler, super-Lee got a 25 percent raise! Figure that one out!

Or how about the CEO of United Airlines? He earned 1200 times more than what a new flight attendant made – in a year when the company's profits fell a whopping 71 percent! Unbelievable!

Okay, so maybe those are the top of the pyramid. But what about the smart and good guys who actually earn their money through the company's increased productivity and performance? Disney's Michael Eisner earns more in one day than the typical Disneyland employee does in an entire year! Come on – where's that at?

By the way – do you know who determines the CEO's pay at these major corporations? The board of directors. And do you know who is the one executive who has the most to do with who gets on that board? You've got that right – the CEO himself!

But hey, that's business – it's not personal.

Right – you mean, like the *business* of government?

Paying for Performance

Tell me, does it make sense to you to raise the pay of congressmen and senators who've been running "U.S.A., Inc." at a loss – nearly a half-trillion dollar loss! – for years? The last year our government took in more money than it spent was 1969– and that's over 20 years ago!

Look, you're a "stockholder" in this country. We all are. How do you feel about the performance of the executives and managers in *your* government? Remember, these guys work for us! And remember, too, these are the people who buy hammers for $650 and toilets for $6000!

Sad, but true – the only time they seem to be able to make a profit is when they use us to make their wars.

Does all this make sense to you?

We pour in money (they call it "taxes"), their performance is at best questionable and they aren't accountable until the next election. So they give themselves a fat raise – and the economy, national debt and balance of trade go all to hell!

It's a scam! – another pyramid scheme! And it's finally falling apart, collapsing, because the value has stopped flowing down to us!

What about Cheating Keating and Company – the whole S & L affair?

Mr. Keating is the guy who was head of now bankrupt Lincoln Savings & Loan, which cost taxpayers $2.6 billion to bail out. They finally put him in jail and then found him guilty of 17 counts of fraud, which could get him 10 years in prison and a fine of $250,000.

And oh, by the way, Keating & Company also donated $1.3 million to the campaign funds of five U.S. Senators. What a coincidence, huh?

How's that for money going up the pyramid and no value coming down?

Problem is, he's the least of the bad news!

More than $250 billion of *our money* down the drain to bail out the failed banks (and more to come) . . . one or two scapegoats in jail (Keating originally faced 77 counts of fraud and racketeering), and we get to pay *increased* taxes to get us out of the mess they created!

So, the government – *our* government – takes over the failed S&Ls. In the third quarter of 1991, the 97 Savings and Loans you and I owned *lost* another $637 million. More than twice what the 2148 solvent, privately owned banks made!!! Now we're talkin'. And these crooks are giving our money away to senators and congressmen!

Talk about pyramids collapsing!
Remember, Ponzi was a banker.

Wall Street and "Greed is Good!"

And how's Michael Milken doing? Remember Mike – king of the junk bonds? We've all read about this man.

This guy has made more than $550 million a year! That's $1.5 million a day!!! And what did he do for all that money? He ripped people off selling them worthless paper he knew was worthless. They're called "junk bonds" for a reason. Now he's doing two to five in a white collar prison, catching up on his reading and learning to meditate. And he'll be out in two years on good behavior with $200 million of O.P.M. (that's "Other People's Money") in his pocket. Would you be willing to spend two years in a federal"country club" pen for $100 million a year?

How about the rest of the "Masters of the Universe" – the "greed is good" guys like in the movie "Wall Street"? Or the real life guys at Salomon Brothers or Drexel Burnham Lambert? You remember, the Ivan Boeskys of the world?

They take our money – yours and mine – millions and millions of dollars of it – and go into bankruptcy with pretty-paper garbage bond investment deals that leverage the leverage they leveraged from the leveraging of the leverage! Folks, the only *real* money involved is ours – not theirs!

The top guys make a killing and everybody else plays dead. This is Monopoly for real! Tell me Wall Street isn't crawling with pyramid schemes and out-

right scams – can you? Seventy years ago they cruci-
fied Carlo Ponzi for doing this stuff – and rightly so!
What else?

How about the *Real* American Dream?

Winning the lottery... we still have *that,* right?

Sure we do. Hey, new millionaires are created
every month in 22 multi-million dollar weekly state
lotteries around the country. And everybody wants to
be one of them. It's legalized gambling and the
government's in on it!

You can even subscribe to magazines that offer to
tell you what to play and how to win! The elderly – the
retired generation on a fixed income – cash their
Social Security checks at the same store that sells
them their tickets. (How's that for irony?) Radio,
television, newspapers and billboards are filled with
ads to play the lottery – paid for by all the people
playing. Incredible! And just about anybody in a big
city can swap food stamps for a chance on this week's
big one.

Look at the lines of people buying lottery tickets –
who's playing? This is crazy! You've got a better
chance of being hit by lightning – twice!

Who's really winning? The government bureacrats
and administrators – the fats cats at the top. Everybody else loses. Isn't that the definition of an illegal
pyramid scheme? Aren't they playing a money-merry-
go-round like Ponzi did?

Nah, it's legal because the government's running it
– and besides, all that money is supposed to go for new
roads and bridges and public schools and . . .

Right. Where's the money really going? Where's

the value flowing? In the words of P.J. O'Rourke, "Giving money and power to the government is like giving whiskey and car keys to teenage boys."

Oh, I almost forgot about two of our favorite sacred cows...

Religion and Education

Jim Bakker and Jimmy Swaggart – these hypocrites infuriate me with their "religious" pyramid schemes.

Hundreds of thousands of people gave them their hope, faith, love and their *money* – and made them mega rich. For what? To make an amusement park out of religion . . . to spend on prostitutes?

There are actually people out there who think money can buy *anything*. These guys had the audacity to stick a "For Sale" sign on the Word of God! Tell me *that's* not a pyramid scheme – illegal, unethical, immoral – you name it!

And education – oh, there's a great one!

Tell me, where else can you invest $40,000, $50,000 or $60,000 and four years or more of your life for a piece of paper that doesn't even guarantee you a decent job? A diploma gets 90 percent of all college grads into a career that lasts, oh, 5 to 10 years – max! That is, if you can find a job at all.

Who gets the good jobs right out of college?

With the exception of the top jocks who turn to pro sports, it's those very, very few at the top of their class in those few top universities – the ones that cost a fortune. Sound a tad exclusive – kinda' like the airplane game? It's a pyramid scheme!

Colleges and universities are big business. And like any business, they should be judged by the quality and success of the product they produce in the marketplace. And if 90 percent of all graduates are not working in what they went to school for in the first place, where's the value flowing down in *that* pyramid?

Remember value for dollars? Do you know what the average college graduate makes today – *if* he or she can even get a job in his or her field of study? Only 500 bucks a week. Now, there's a great return on investment!

Take away the fat endowments – Harvard $4.65 billion, Yale $2.57 billion, Princeton $2.53 billion – are most colleges and universities profitable? If you made them operate like a real business, most would be bankrupt in a year!

General vs. Specific Education

Now don't get me wrong. I'm not knocking a college education. I truly believe that if everybody in North America had a college degree, we'd be living in a kinder, gentler world.

College definitely makes people more well-rounded. More aware. And usually more confident. As a good friend of mine put it, "College gives you peripheral vision – you see things in a larger context, you learn how to solve problems."

That pretty well sums it up. But as Napoleon Hill pointed out in his classic book, *Think and Grow Rich:*

"There are two kinds of knowledge. One is general, the other is specialized. General knowledge, no matter how great in quantity or variety it may be, is of but little use in the accumulation of money."

I went to college and I'm glad I did. But the real purpose of a general college education is to improve peoples' vision and to provide a bridge — let me repeat, a BRIDGE — between the home and the big, wide world. (And let's face it, after 18 years most parents want their kids out of the house so bad they'll even pay for their education!)

In reality, college is not the best training for a career unless it's *specialized training* to become a doctor or engineer or accountant or the like. That's why Network Marketing is such a powerful vehicle for earning income. It's a *specialized system* for wealth creation without a $40,000 investment and four years of hard work just to start earning your first dollar!

Illusion vs. Reality

Most people are under the illusion that they'll graduate from college and walk right into a solid career opportunity.

It's like the story of the man who died and went to Purgatory.

The archangel in charge explained to the man that he could choose between going to Heaven or Hell, but once he made the choice — that was it. The man asked if he could see them both before he made his final choice. The archangel said, "Sure."

When they got to Heaven, it was beautiful. Everybody was smiling. It was peaceful and tranquil — just perfect. The people seemed content and so happy. It certainly looked very lovely indeed.

"This is beautiful," the man said. "May I see the other now?" The archangel took him down to Hell.

It was incredible — one huge party! People were laughing and dancing, the music was blaring. There was a lavish spread of magnificent food, everybody was drinking and carrying on. The man had never seen anything like it in his life and his eyes were as big as silver dollars.

The archangel leaned over to him and asked, "Well, which do you choose?"

"Oh, this one – this one!" Said the man excitedly. "I want to be in Hell."

The archangel reminded the man that he only had one choice. "Are you certain you want to be in Hell?" He asked him. "Oh, yes – I'm positive."

The archangel clapped his hands and in a flash, the music stopped, the party disappeared and the man found himself chained to a post with flames shooting at him from every direction.

"No!" he cried to another suffering soul. "Where did the party go – the people, the dancing, all the food?"

"Oh," said the soul, "You must have attended the opportunity meeting. This is what hell is *really* like."

The moral of the story? Things are not always what they appear to be – just ask the college graduates who had to move back home because they couldn't find a job! What college is best at preparing people for is – you got it, *more college*. Get a degree, then another and another. You, too, can become a professional student. In 1960, we graduated 9,733 Ph.D.s. Today, more than 36,000 each year! Where do they all go?

The academic lifestyle – it's a world unto itself. Really, where's the value flowing? Nowhere! It's all bottled up in the university where it stays because if they let it out – we wouldn't need them anymore, would we?

Once college professors work their way up the academic ladder to the safety and security of "tenure," they get to do research and publish a book that nobody reads– much less understands. And if you've been watching the news lately, you'll see that if they're in any one of the high-tech fields, they'll most likely be doing research for Hitachi or Mitsubishi – so that the Japanese get another patent on an American invention!

No wonder Japan is eating America's lunch in the marketplace!

Folks, it's time we all took a reality check. Let's face it, when you try to use your B.S. degree to achieve financial independence, you'll find out what "BS" really stands for – "Back to School" – because that's where you'll head when you can't find a job.

■ ■ ■

CHAPTER SIX

There Is No Security Anymore

Why a chapter on security?

Because security is what people want most. All the research shows that it continues to top the list of what people desire in their careers, for their families and for their futures, too.

The unhappy truth of life in America today is that *security* is slipping away – or gone – for most of us. And it's going at an alarming rate.

But security is the cornerstone of The American Dream – isn't it?

The fact is, there is no more security in the old, antiquated way of doing business.

Just ask the former employees of Eastern Airlines. Or Pan Am. Or scores of other workers who have been laid off from "blue chip" companies that are bankrupt or restructuring.

Even in the face of the most massive layoffs since the Great Depression, people still think they can find security by working for a traditional business. It reminds me of a story.

I'm Sticking to My Story

One night a guy decided to drop by a local bar after work to have a drink with his friends. Everybody was having a great time! Swapping stories . . . singing along with the juke box . . . buying rounds of drinks for the table.

Before he knew it, he and his friends had closed the place down. As he stumbled to his car, he could see the sun breaking over the horizon. He glanced at his watch. 6:00 a.m. "Oh, no, " he thought to himself. "I've done it again. My wife will kill me . . . I promised her no more all night binges!"

Twenty minutes later he pulled into the driveway, rehearsing the excuse he thought up on the way home. As he stumbled through the front door, he looked up to see his wife waiting for him with her arms crossed.

"Where have you been all night?" she demanded. He straightened up, looked her right in the eye and slurred, "I got home just after midnight, and I didn't want to wake you . . . so I slept in the hammock outside." His wife glared at him and responded. "Nice try . . . only one problem . . . we took the hammock down two years ago!"

The man gave her a startled look and then blurted, *"Well, that's my story and I'm sticking to it!"*

My friend, people who think they can have the same job security in the 1990's that workers enjoyed in the 1950's are just kidding themselves . . . they're telling themselves a lie . . . and sticking to it.

In the words of President Bush, "Read my lips!" There is no job security anymore. It's time to tell yourself the truth . . . prepare yourself to face the consequences . . . and get on with your life!

A Brave New World?

Today, it takes at least two incomes for us to achieve the standard of living our parents had with one income. And even that's a stretch: now, people are talking about the *three-income* family as if that were normal!

Things are changing so fast in our world and workplace that people who had iron-clad, life-long positions with solid companies just a few short years ago are out of work today.

The 1980s saw 30 percent of all Americans lose their jobs – 30 percent! They were mostly blue collar people displaced or replaced by automation and advanced technology, as entire industries were transformed seemingly overnight. By the end of this decade, we could see 35 percent of existing white collar workers unemployed as well. The figure is currently at 700,000 or more jobs lost per year – that's 2690 jobs ended, gone forever, every business day! We're talking monthly unemployment figures of 1,500,000! Remember what economist Pilzer predicted – 20 percent unemployment by the year 2000!

Most of us can accept that certain industries are born, grow, prosper, get old and eventually die. That's just the way it is. And it's foolish to hang on to the past and fight progress.

Around the turn of the century, we were a land of farmers. Ninety percent of the population was involved in producing the food we needed as a nation. Today, three percent of us produce not only all that we require in America, but an additional 20 percent above that – which we sell or give to the rest of the world! The sons of farmers today are computer programmers, chemical engineers and lawyers – not farmers. Why should they be? There's no security in farming anymore – and certainly no opportunity or money, either.

Steel workers, auto workers, machinists – the jobs of so many tradesmen and women our economy depended upon just 20 or even 10 short years ago – are disappearing *fast*. Technological advances leading to higher productivity at a substantially lower cost are required for businesses to remain competitive in today's marketplace.

Industries that hang onto workers they don't really need may be looked upon as kinder and gentler, but not when they're forced out of business and into bankruptcy because they couldn't compete.

It just doesn't make sense to continue to pay three workers $30,000 a year each if they can be replaced by a machine that costs $50,000 – a machine that never takes a vacation, doesn't go on strike for higher wages, doesn't require a benefit package with a pension and will never file a sexual harassment law suit.

I mentioned vinyl records before. Now there was a solid, secure, mega-million dollar business that was on top of the world just six or seven years ago. To tell you the truth, if I told you back in 1985 there would be no record industry in 1990 – you'd have laughed me out of the room, wouldn't you? Today, cassette tapes and compact disks have made vinyl records virtually obsolete.

The owners, executives, managers, shareholders, workers – and all the lawyers, insurance companies, equipment manufacturers, construction workers, suppliers, vendors, service companies, etc., who depended upon the vinyl record industry for their livelihoods, have either gone someplace else for work . . . are unemployed . . . or went out of business.

And hey, the music business itself is better than ever!

Recording artists are flourishing. So are the "record" companies – CDs have doubled their sales dollars! One person's prosperity can often come at the cost of another's security.

Get an Education

Going to college, getting a good job, providing a secure future for yourself and your family isn't what it used to be. It's a myth, isn't it?

Sure, they teach you a lot in college. But none of the professors teach you how to become financially secure. It reminds me of a poem by Stephen Crane, the author of *The Red Badge of Courage:*

I met a seer.
He held in his hands
The book of wisdom.
"Sir," I addressed him,
"Let me read."
"Child –" he began.
"Sir," I said,
"Think not that I am a child,
For already I know much
Of that which you hold.
Aye much."

He smiled.
Then he opened the book
And held it before me –
Strange that I should have
grown so suddenly blind.

The "book of wisdom" that tells you how to achieve The American Dream doesn't exist in any college library. Even if it did, only a very few college students would be able to understand a word of it.

The job market for college grads is the worst in over 20 years! The baby boom that created the most awesome market for goods and services the world has ever seen... that created the most massive block of college graduates... also created the most cut-throat, competitive job market ever!

Get a Job

We've lost as many as a quarter of a million jobs in a single month – and that figure is destined to get higher and higher – and that doesn't include the millions of people whose jobless benefits have run out... who've given up and quit looking for work!

The number of men and women changing jobs every year now is astonishing! It used to be that you'd get into an industry and there you'd stay 'til you retired. Maybe you'd make one change. But today, employment experts *expect* people to have 10 to 12 different *careers* in their working lives! Where's the security in that?

Even the U.S. military is laying people off! Officers – from lieutenants to generals – are being offered cash payments to take early retirement. Why? Because the Army doesn't need them and can't afford to pay them.

The cold war was hot business for the defense industry. But all the businesses that supplied weapons and uniforms and supplies to the military are paying a big price for peace – they're laying off thousands of workers!

How would you like to be in the defense industry today?

No matter where you turn – with very, very few exceptions – there simply is no more security in the American workplace today.

Free enterprise is no longer *free*. Most people don't have that most American of all rights, a choice. They have to take what they can get. There's no freedom in that – and no security, either.

The Wonderful World of Conventional Small Business Ownership

Remember, more than 90 percent of all conventional small businesses fail within the first five years. Of the 10 percent that make it through, very few will ever see year ten. How many ten-year-old businesses do you know of?

The truth is that most small business entrepreneurs don't own their own businesses – they own their own *jobs!* I know. I had my own business when I was 24-years old. I got fed up and I quit working for someone else and went to work for myself. Unfortunately, I quickly found out that I was like the lawyer who has himself for a client – I was working for a crazy person! I put in one frantic year of 80 plus hour weeks ... made a million dollars, in fact ... but I spent almost a million and a half bucks doing it. Now that's an expensive education!

I can hear you now, "Maybe you should have gone to college, Burke." Well, I did that, too. I've got a college degree in criminal justice to prove it. Hey, you wouldn't happen to have a job for a prison warden in training, would you? Trust me, it's not the best vehicle for becoming financially independent!

Franchising

Many people today turn to franchising as an alternative to starting their own high risk business from scratch.

To get into the franchise business, you pay money in the form of a licensing fee to a franchisor who hands you what's called a "turn-key" business operation. Everything is already researched, developed, designed and set up for you – from advertising to the proper equipment to use. You learn how to train your people, do your books, make your products, get your supplies, and so on. You just pay your money, turn the key and drive off into the sunset of success, right? Wrong.

One major problem – when you add up the costs of leasing your space, remodeling it, buying the equipment, paying for inventory, etc. . . . . the average franchise costs $85,000 to get started!

What's more you've got a seven-day week of 12 to 14 hour days managing a bunch of minimum wage employees. And, if you're very good, after three to five years you'll break even and be able to start making a profit. Most owner-operated franchises today provide about a $50,000 to $60,000 annual income for the owner once the initial investment's all paid off – if the owner doesn't rely too heavily on support management staff.

You can earn more if you can afford one of the bigger and better ones. McDonalds franchises are virtually fail-safe. But you'll pay a steep price for your profits. A McDonalds franchise costs more than $1 million dollars to get off the ground!

Did you know that one third of all franchisees loses their shirts . . .one third just breaks even . . .and one third makes a profit?

That means 66 out of every 100 are losers! It's better odds than the lottery, but with the price of the franchise ticket averaging $85,000, it should be!

Experienced, professional franchisees today will tell you that unless you're going to own a string of five or more – forget it. You might as well save yourself the headaches and heartaches and stick with your job.

Help!

The simple fact is, we cannot depend on help from the outside.

Somebody once said that "Hope is the expectation that something or somebody is going to come along and save your butt." There is no hope for most people. The institutions of education, government and business can no longer be counted on to provide us with the opportunity to accomplish our dreams.

We have to take matters into our own hands. And what that means in the simplest of terms is – *if it's meant to be, it's up to me.* For things to change – you have to change. For things to get better – you have to get better.

So, what are you going to do?

What *can* you do?

■ ■ ■

CHAPTER SEVEN

What Are Your Options?

Okay, let's say that you accept the fact that there's no security in the work world anymore . . . and that, "If it's going to be – it's up to me." Where do you go . . .? What are you going to do . . .?

Here Are Your Options:

A Job: That's the trading time for money trap we talked about before. No matter what you earn, there's neither security nor freedom in having a job. That's putting your life in someone else's hands.

Zig Ziglar, one of America's top sales motivators, once described the word JOB as "Just – Over – Broke." And in today's changing work world, the only for sure jobs are the few and far between ones at the very top – or those menial jobs at the very bottom.

Self-Employment: That's where most people will turn. However, as we've said, the odds are stacked against you even for starting up the most modest of conventional small businesses.

If you're one of the few who make it past the first couple of years, you've got a chance. You can shift the odds in your favor with a franchise . . . if you've got the cash . . . or if you're willing to hock your parent's house or your first-born child and risk going into very deep debt. Either way – good luck to you.

Investments: This one works great. It's how the rich got rich and how they continue to get richer. You can earn an income of $5000 a month with about half a million dollars in investments. A million or so bucks invested in the right place will give you $100,000 a year income. All you need is the cash capital to start with. Unfortunately, most of us weren't born with the last name of Rockefeller, Vanderbilt, or Kennedy.

There's One More Way

It's the way to earn money that successful authors, songwriters, musicians, actors and performing artists use. You can find work that pays *residual income*, also known as "passive income" – or "royalties."

Sadly, very few of us have a bestselling book or record or brilliant invention in us. Only a very elite group of people have the God-given gift to be the next Stephen King or Michael Jackson.

But you know what? There is a way that you – whoever you are, whatever your sex or race or family background or social status... whatever your education or past history of success or failure in any endeavor – can begin to earn enduring, residual income *right now, today!*

It's called Network Marketing.

And before you say – or think – another thing, I want you to give me a chance.... No – scratch that – I want *you* to *make the chance **for yourself*** to take a look at Network Marketing and see what it has to offer you.

You've Got Everything to Gain

We've seen how our entire world today is filled with pyramids: good ones, bad ones, legal ones and illegal ones. Doesn't the fact that all these businesses and social and cultural institutions – like schools, colleges, government and churches, even families – are all multi-level pyramids tell you something interesting?

Good or bad has nothing to do with the fundamental structure or shape – does it? It's what people do with it – how they apply the natural pyramid principle of value flowing down in direct proportion to power (in the form of dollars or votes) flowing up that makes the difference.

What does that mean for you? Just this: how you make use of what's available to you is your choice.

And I say, the best possible choice you could make today is Network Marketing.

I'm going to show you and tell you what Network Marketing is and what it is *not*.

I want you to understand this business. I want you to compare it to all the other ways of earning a living we've talked about and see how it measures up.

I want you to look at Network Marketing and see if it will provide you the security and freedom you need to capture and keep your American Dream.

You've got nothing to lose.

And if what I say about Network Marketing is true – think for just a moment about what you might have to gain....

■ ■ ■

Phase Three:

Why Traditional Ways
Aren't Working Anymore
■

CHAPTER EIGHT

Paradigm – A $100 Word and a Million Dollar Idea

Do you know what a "paradigm" is? It's one of those $100 college words that actually has a pretty simple meaning. A paradigm is a point of view or a model, kind of like the status quo, the way we see the world around us – "the way it is."

The American Dream is a paradigm – only for most of us today, it's the way it *was* – not the way it is.

Here's a good example of what paradigms are – and how they change.

The Swiss Watch Paradigm

Do you remember what the standard was – the operating paradigm – for watch-making back about 25 years ago? The Swiss watch, right? It was Rolex and the like: classic, accurate, 17 jewels, a mainspring to wind up, tick-tick-tick-tick-tick....

Now, one day, this little old Swiss watchmaker comes running out of his shop jumping up and down about this neat, new watch he'd just made.

"Look, Wolfgang – no mainspring, no jewels. It's lighter and a whole lot cheaper to make. It's thinner and you never have to wind it. And – it's a hundred times more accurate! It's called a quartz!"

Well, the Swiss are a pretty cautious and conservative bunch. So their first response was to lean back, puff on their pipes and say,

"Hold on now, Fritz – not so fast. This quartz thing is pretty clever. But look, if we start making these quartz watches, then who's gonna want these big expensive 17 jewel jobs we make now. We'll be competing against ourselves.

"We've got millions invested in jewels and gears and springs and things. What are we going to do with all of that stuff – throw it away? And what are we going to do with all the little old watchmakers – like you? Besides, we OWN the watch business now. We're the kings of the mountain. Why mess with success? Let's not fix what's not broken."

The Swiss Watch Paradigm – that's the way it was.

See, the Swiss didn't think quartz technology would amount to much. So, instead of rocking their own boat, they sold it – to the Japanese.

You remember the Japanese 35 years ago – those guys who made all that cheap stuff that broke 10 minutes after you bought it? The guys who were suckers for any new fangled high-tech gizmo? "Made in Japan" – Ha ha ha!

Ha ha, indeed. Who owns the watch market now? The Japanese and their quartz watches.

We didn't just switch watches – we changed paradigms.

Move over Rolex – Here Comes Seiko

The last time the Swiss had a really big hit in the watch business was "Swatch." Cheap, light, cute, bright – and quartz! They copied them from the Japanese!

See, a paradigm – the way it is – becomes "the way it was" when it doesn't work anymore. Or when somebody invents a new, better paradigm to take its place.

Right now for example, the old paradigm of The American Dream has stopped working for all but a very, very few.

We know that's true by answering one simple question: Do you have it? Is it working for you? Are you living The American Dream right now?

If you're not, you're not alone. You're part of a mega-group that's been given a new definition of "middle" class – you're in the *middle* between a rock and a hard place.

Now, don't get caught in the trap of saying something like, "Well, I just don't work hard enough..." Or, "I'm just not smart enough...."

Tell me the God's honest truth – if you worked twice as hard as you do now, would that really make a difference? Would you be earning twice as much?

And do you really need to be twice as smart as you are right now to make it in this world – to be a success? Look around: the "A" students are working for the "C" students. Being two or three times smarter isn't the answer either. If intelligence were the answer, college professors would be the wealthiest people in the world – and you know that's not the way it is.

If you're like most people I know, you probably believe the reason you don't have The American Dream is because you didn't take all the right steps you were supposed to take. You probably think you got off track somewhere – that you're missing something – and if you only had it, you'd have your Dream and be able to live it, too. Is that true?

Well, my friends, *you* are not missing anything.

What's missing is a new American Dream paradigm – one that works. Because the old one has fallen apart.

Who Stole The American Dream?

Who stole the American Dream? The fat cats at the top of corporate America – that's who. The CEO's who are making millions while their companies are losing money – that's who!

The reason you don't have The American Dream, and millions of other people just like you don't have it – the reason I didn't used to have it, either – is that there are a bunch of greedy guys out there with a vested interest in keeping it all for themselves. And the best way to do that is to make sure you don't get it.

Look, if you were king of the mountain, would you really want to rock the boat? Would you risk being the one on top just to try something new? Or would you be like the guys who owned the Swiss watch business and hold tight until that foolish quartz thing blew over?

Remember, people generally resist change. And the comfort zone is all the more comfortable when you're rich and famous – when you're the one who's king.

What Walt Disney was talking about when he said it took courage to pursue your dreams was having the courage to accept change – the courage to climb aboard a new and better idea *before* everybody else

does . . . because if you wait 'til everyone is doing it –
it's too late!

By the time regular people get into a hot real estate
market . . . or by the time the stock market hits a new
high, the big money's already been made. The experts
are long gone and all that's left for the ordinary guys
and gals are the crumbs.

The new and better paradigm I'm talking about –
the way *you* can get back The American Dream – is not
the college and a career track paradigm – like it used
to be.

Not the job with corporate America paradigm – like
it used to be.

Not the owning your own small business paradigm,
either.

Believe me, I tried them all. And I didn't make it in
any of them. I made it in the *new and better* paradigm
of Network Marketing.

College, corporate jobs, even small business owner-
ship – they're all old paradigm stuff. Swiss watches.
Dead and dying dinosaurs.

The Technology of Network Marketing

Network Marketing is the quartz technology of
business today. Because Network Marketing has
what's missing from conventional business.

And what's that?

In one word – *technology*.

And what's that mean?

Technology is simply "a new and better way of
doing something."

Technology is the engine of change.

Technology is what creates a new paradigm.

Today, technology is causing things that used to

take 50 years to change . . . to happen in only five! And that's very good news because it's clearly time for a change for the better – a dramatic change that will affect the way that America and the world does business from now on!

■ ■ ■

CHAPTER NINE

Why Network Marketing? Ch...ch...ch...Changes

The most fundamental fact of life in our world today is change.

And as a rule, people are reluctant to change. We resist it. It has to do with staying in our comfort zone, which is part of human nature.

But it's also true that what you resist – persists. And when you push against a change whose time has come – it resists big time!

Enlightenment versus "En-darkenment"

Throughout human history, as changes have come to light, people have run around blowing out candles and throwing the switches, demanding continued darkness. In almost every field of endeavor – the arts, sciences, medicine, business – most new ideas have met with resistance and rejection at first. And the more unique and revolutionary the idea, the more sweeping and vast the change, the louder and stronger people's opposition to it.

Now, you can understand why people in the Dark ages or even in the 17th, 18th and 19th centuries were afraid and even ignorant about change. They threw

Copernicus in jail. Ridiculed Christopher Columbus. Laughed at Louis Pasteur. Even mocked Edison and Einstein. But you know, even today, we still resist change.

Let's look at some recent examples.

The Buying and Selling of America

Once upon a time, back in the 1800s, America bought what it needed at small, family owned shops like the general store. It was the butcher, the baker and the candle-stick maker paradigm.

Then, a man named W.T. Grant had a very bright idea. What if we combined all these separate, little shops by making them individual departments under one roof–in one big store? Then, we put one store over here, then one there... offer our customers the widest selection at lowest prices because we buy the stuff from the manufacturers at the biggest volume discounts, and – bingo – the 5 & 10 Cent department store chain was born. A new and better way of doing things. A brand new technology creating a new and better shopping paradigm.

And people flocked to it.

Can you guess what happened next?

Making Money the Old Fashioned Way

The individual merchants who owned those other "old fashioned" retail stores were unhappy people, to say the least. They saw their business drop to next to nothing as more and more people sought the wider selection, lower prices and greater convenience of the local 5 & 10 Cent department store.

The old-fashioned "mom and pop" stores were dropping like flies.

Well, those shop keepers didn't take it lying down – no sir! They fought back. However, they didn't fight back with a new and better idea themselves. They held on to the old paradigm and fought back *politically*.

Since there were thousands and thousands of them (with thousands and thousands of votes), they lobbied hard and fast for their right to do things the same old way. And they got the local and state governments to outlaw Grant's 5 & 10 Cent department stores.

Did you know that? Imagine, 5 & 10 Cent store chains throughout the country were *illegal!* Incredible!

Eventually, Grant's department stores won out. Remember, what you resist – persists. You'd have better luck standing in front of an oncoming freight train than to fight against a change to a new and better way of doing things whose time has come – especially when consumers love the idea.

Shopping Centers and Malls

After the chain department stores took over the major market share in consumer goods retailing – the smaller merchants finally came to their senses and embraced the new technology. They began to look for innovative ways to use it themselves.

As the automobile made growing suburbs out of near-city farm land, groups of merchants got together in a collective way and formed shopping centers – a variety of individual stores all in the same, convenient location. The zoning battles that followed – fueled by all the shop owners who didn't get into the new shopping centers – were nasty indeed.

Eventually, shopping centers, too, proliferated. And before long, developers enclosed them and put roofs over them – kind of like what the chain department stores had done initially – and called them shopping "malls."

They became a way of life in North America.

Yet today, both department stores and malls are becoming old and dying paradigms.

Department stores are now losing the battle they won 50 years ago. Specialty shops and discount stores are eating their lunch. Visits to chain department stores went from 65 percent of all consumers on a per month basis in 1974, down to 47 percent in 1990. The number of shoppers visiting *discount stores* was up 65 percent in the same period.

Malls are suffering a similar fate. As retailers raise the profit per square foot through their own new and better technologies, the need for retail outlets is decreasing. The average profit per square foot for a retailer is $125. Yet specialty retailers are making $400 per square foot – that's over three time more profitable! Which means the demand for traditional retail stores – like J.C. Penneys, Sears and Montgomery Wards – is decreasing.

Today, there are too many malls. And the ones that remain are having to do more and more to attract the same number of shoppers as before.

What technology will retailers incorporate to make malls new and better? How about the mall as a theme park – shopping as entertainment? Check out Century City in L.A. – or even better, Canada's Edmonton Mall – the Disneyland of malls.

Edmonton Mall. Wow! A shopping mall that's 115 football fields in size and houses the world's largest indoor amusement park, indoor wave pool and indoor golf course! There's a fleet of operable submarines bigger than the Canadian Navy, a full size replica of Christopher Columbus' Santa Maria and – oh yes – nearly 1000 individual stores!

How's that for power shopping?! That's what it takes to make a mall that works today. Unfortunately, even a "Hollywood-comes-to-the-mall" approach can't guarantee success – at last report Edmonton Mall is struggling!

It's tough to compete when your paradigm is sinking.

Franchising

One of the most amazing innovations in how America buys and sells what it wants was – and still is – franchising.

You know, 30 years ago franchising was a revolutionary new technology – a new and better way to retail goods, food products and services to the consumer.

And boy did people hate it! Resistance, big time.

Newspapers and magazines shouted bold headlines about what a scam and rip-off franchising was. Stories of little old ladies who lost their life savings to some flim-flam franchise were everywhere.

Even though some very big, well known Fortune 500 type companies were involved, those companies insisted that their names not be used in ads or magazine stories – even about their own franchises! There was actually a *very* strong move in Congress to outlaw franchising altogether.

Today – this once shaky, shady, so-called scam is responsible for over 34 percent of all retail sales in America. Franchises sell $758,500,000,000 worth of goods and services – *that's 758.5 billion dollars!*

Franchising was simply a new technology. Clearly, a revolutionary, very powerful, and very, very successful technology – a new and better method for the distribution and sales of goods and services.

Is there a new, emerging distribution and sales technology on the horizon that'll out perform franchising?

Is there a new next step in the evolution of our free enterprise system?

Yes, there is.

The New Technology of Distribution and Sales

It's called Network Marketing.

And even more than department store chains, shopping centers, malls and franchising that came before, Network Marketing has been resisted. It's been misunderstood, criticized, laughed at and lobbied and legislated against.

The Pioneers

Just look at Amway, the granddaddy of all Network Marketing companies. Amway distributors have been mocked . . . laughed at . . . and derided since the company burst onto the scene over thirty years ago.

Today, Amway is a multi-billion dollar a year company with successful distributors all over the world.

Now, let me set the record straight – I'm not an Amway distributor. And I'm not endorsing their opportunity. My first, last and only commitment is to all the companies in the entire industry.

The Network Marketing industry owes Amway a debt of gratitude. They were the first major players in a revolutionary experiment . . . they were the Model-T Ford version of a brave new industry. It's because of them that major companies are now involved (and more are becoming involved everyday) in Network Marketing.

Network Marketing has come a long way from the first Model-T. In fact, today's companies look more like Formula One racers than Model-T's! Which is why the new Network Marketing of the 90's is such a powerful vehicle for financial independence.

I'm convinced we will see history repeat itself here.

I'm convinced Network Marketing will surpass the astounding success of department stores and franchises . . .that Network Marketing will revolutionize the way America buys and sells *everything!*

Why? Look around. It's already happening.

■ ■ ■

CHAPTER TEN

Whisper This Word to Yourself:
"Distribution"

In his landmark book, *Unlimited Wealth,* noted economist Paul Zane Pilzer asks us to recall a memorable scene from the 1960's movie *The Graduate.* In the film Dustin Hoffman plays the part of Ben, a recent college graduate. One evening at a party, an older, wiser man pulls Ben aside and promises to share the secret to the future with him. He whispers in his ear one precious word, *"Plastics."*

In the 1990s, Paul Pilzer, whispers a different, though no less profound and magic word in our ears: *"Distribution."*

Here's why.

The Technology of Distribution

The most visible and powerful impact technology has had to date on the goods and services we buy is in reducing the cost of making a product. And it's a proven *marketing law* that when you lower the price, you sell much, much more.

Not many Americans owned calculators when they sold for $125. When the retail price fell below $20 – every body had one – then two. The same was true for digital watches and a whole host of products.

Look what happened to VCRs.

At $1,000 plus – the affluent were the only ones who owned them. Today, at $300 to $400, 68 percent of all households have one. By 1995 that figure is projected to be 85 percent. And for your $350, today's VCRs have more features and a higher level of all-around quality than even the most sophisticated 1980s models.

Pick a product – any product – and you'll find the same thing has happened. Adjust the dollars for inflation, and today you've got six or seven times the value, quality, features, safety and longevity that you could purchase 20 or even 10 short years ago.

A top model color TV, with automatic color control and a 15 inch screen, cost $300 in the 1970s. Today, $300 buys you the same size set, cable ready, with remote control, electronic tuning, and a far superior color picture. In 1989 $300 would be about $120 in 1970's money – adjusting for inflation. So, today you not only get a far better TV set, but it also costs 60 percent less!

Refrigerators, automobiles, computers... they're all the same. Advances in technology, i.e. new and better ways of doing things – in this case, of making things – have slashed the retail prices, and sales have increased accordingly.

When the price comes down, then what was once a luxury all of a sudden becomes a necessity. Everybody has to have one. When TVs became cheap enough, everybody went out and bought one.

The next step was having two – one for the living room and another for the bedroom. From 1960 to

1980, the number of homes owning a TV set only increased from 90 to 98 percent, while those owning two sets, rose from 11 to 60 percent! Now, let's have one in the kitchen, too. If that's not enough, some hotels have a T.V. in every bathroom!

Once you have all the TVs you need and want what's next?

Better quality.

The one in the living room gets replaced with a big-screen, stereo job. And on and on it goes. From Sony Walkmans, to automobiles, to suits, shoes and cocktail dresses – first comes quantity, then comes quality. And since technology is constantly producing new and better ways of making things – and new and better things themselves – there are always new and better products for new and bigger markets.

That, my friends, is what makes America – and what will keep America – the leader of the world.

We are the world's biggest market for just about *everything*. They (the Japanese, Germans and any other of *them*) may giggle behind our backs... make snide remarks about "materialistic Americans," but never for too long. They not only know which side their bread is buttered on – they know who's got the bread!

Why Does Everything Cost So Much?

Okay, now, how come some things haven't come down in price? Food, for example.

Great question – and food is the perfect example.

The cost of making most food products was lowered to rock bottom by new and better growing and production technologies many years ago.

How much does it cost for the wheat in a box of Wheaties? Five cents – or less? But the darn thing is selling for $2.50 or more! That's because the biggest cost of the product isn't in the manufacturing. And it's not in the packaging, either, which only adds another dime. It's in the *distribution and sales.*

It used to be that a product's production cost was around 50 percent of its retail price Not any more. Advances in manufacturing technology – all the way from the cost of farming or mining the raw materials themselves through producing the finished product – has dropped that cost down to less than 10 to 20 percent of the finished product's price. Food is typically 15 percent. Clothing 17 percent. The "cost-of-goods" is about as low as it's going to go across the board.

But at the same time manufacturing costs were being cut way down, the costs of distribution and sales were climbing higher and higher. Today, those expenses represent about 80 to 90 percent of what a consumer pays for a product at retail.

Now, if you want to be the most competitive guy with the lowest price, which are you going to do? (A) Focus your efforts on reducing the already rock-bottom cost of making it? Or (B) Go after the 80 to 90 percent it costs to distribute and sell it? (B) – obviously.

Saving 10 to 20 percent off the 15 cent cost of production doesn't show up very much in the reduced retail dollar. But take 20 percent out of the *85 cent cost* of distribution and sales and that's a very big deal – for both producers and consumers.

And if you want proof, just ask the richest man in America – Sam Walton.

America's Real Uncle Sam

Sam and his family own Walmart, easily the most successful distributor of merchandise in all of North America and, therefore, in all the world.

Just how successful is Walmart?

When the Walton family sits down together for Sunday dinner, the collective net worth of the people at that table is $22 *billion* – give or take a couple of hundred million!!!

Experts predict that by the mid-1990s, Walmart will overtake Sears to become the biggest retailer in tne world. By the way, Walmart is still primarily just a regional company. They only opened their first stores outside the Southern U.S. in the last couple of years!

And what does this real, live "Uncle Sam" and his Walmart stores do for a living?

They distribute and sell other peoples' products. In fact, they don't actually "sell" anything. They just make the best selling models and brands available as part of the widest selection in one convenient location at the absolute cheapest price in town. The old joke goes: "How do you find the local Walmart store? It's right across from a boarded up K-mart." Yes, they are that good!

Distribution – that's the key.

If you can develop a new and better method – a better technology for distributing goods and services than most businesses are using today – you will be very, very rich tomorrow.

And the good news is, you don't have to design and develop that new and better method of distribution and sales all by yourself. Because it's here, up and working, right now. What's more, it's been successfully tested, refined and proven for more than 50 years in the marketplace.

As for getting rich doing it – just ask Jay Van Andel and Rich DeVos.

These two were on *Forbes* magazine's 1991 list of the richest people in America. Each man is worth $2.9 billion. In fact, they have the fastest growing fortune's on the list. And they're breathing down Sam Walton's neck because *they* are the future of sales and distribution.

Van Andel and DeVos are the founders of Amway, one of the most successful Network Marketing companies in the world.

And they started in the exact same place you have the opportunity to begin – as independent Network Marketers... men and women who have, right at their fingertips, the latest leading-edge technology that's revolutionizing the sales and distribution of virtually every consumer product and service in the world!

■ ■ ■

Phase Four:

The Truth About Network Marketing
■

CHAPTER ELEVEN

What Is Network Marketing?

It *really* used to bother me when someone would say, "Network Marketing is a pyramid scheme." I mean, look at what we've revealed about government, corporate America, colleges and universities – all those good old American institutions that are ripping people off in a big way *and getting away with it.*

Sure, Network Marketing is a multi-level pyramid. But remember, *everything* that distributes goods and services is a pyramid. What matters is whether value flows down through the levels of the pyramid in direct proportion to the dollars that flow back up. Consumers need to end up with a quality product or service, at a reasonable price – bona fide *distribution.*

Now, I'm not saying Network Marketing is pure and perfect. People fail in this business, too. Just like they fail in school or drop out of college. And by the way, look at the world – do you see more people failing or succeeding?

The 80-20 rule applies to Network Marketing – just as it applies to real estate sales and government jobs and everything else: 20% of the people do 80% of the work.

It's absolutely true that Networking companies make mistakes . . . some even do downright stupid things. Some products don't cut it in the marketplace. When the value stops flowing down, any pyramid collapses – legal or illegal. And yes, there have been people who abuse the concept and make it dirty. Sadly, there are Michael Milkens and Jim Bakkers in every business.

Remember the analogy about sex that I used before? There's making love and there's abuse and rape. It's not that sex itself is bad. It's how people use it.

It's the same with anything – and yes, Network Marketing, too.

You see, when it's all said and done, Network Marketing is quite an unconventional approach to distribution and sales. That's why the timing couldn't be better to become involved right now. And that doesn't sit well with people who've got their hearts and minds – and wallets – heavily invested in keeping the status quo – the same-old conventional way of doing things. You think the guys in the vinyl record business had great things to say about compact disk technology when they first saw it?

If you want to catch major flack in this world, go out and do something in a new and better way – then *duck!* Nay-sayers are everywhere. (I wonder who pays those guys!)

The Power of the Pyramid

Just for fun, take out a U.S. one dollar bill. Turn it over. Look at the left hand side. What do you see? A pyramid!

The founders of our country recognized the pyramid as a strong, enduring structure. According to geometry, the strongest of all. Wide at the bottom and growing narrower at the top – able to support great weight and stand for ages against the natural elements.

The "Founding Fathers" of our country were Freemasons, a brotherhood of builders. And in this case, a group of nation builders who created the world's first real democracy founded on the principles of equal opportunity, freedom of choice, freedom of speech and free enterprise.

The Latin mottos above and below the pyramid say: *Annuit Cœptis,* which means: "God has favored our undertaking." And, *Novus Ordo Seclorum,* which means, "A new order of the ages."

Interesting, isn't it? The United States of America – a pyramid! And if ever there was a pure and perfect, democratic example of the best of free enterprise, it's Network Marketing.

The Power of Networking – Christianity

Perhaps the most extraordinary example of the power of Networking is Christianity.

About two thousand years ago, Jesus Christ appeared with a compelling message about a new and better way of doing things. He gathered around him a small core group of people – average folks: fishermen, tax collectors, teenagers... who caught the vision, who shared his dream. He spoke to individuals, small groups and large gatherings. The word spread.

Yet even among his ardent believers and followers, there was one who betrayed him and others who denied and doubted, too. But no matter, for Jesus had taken a stand for a new way of living that was unshakable. It was such a powerful commitment that it extended long after he physically left this earth.

Now, almost 2000 years later, that handful of believers has conveyed the message of Jesus Christ by word-of-mouth down through centuries to vastly more people than that small, original group probably ever dreamed possible – today more than 25 percent of the population on this planet are Christians . . . that's over one and a quarter billion people!

The spread of Christianity throughout the world was accomplished by many of the same principles we find operating today in Network Marketing: word-of-mouth or person-to-person recommendations . . . testimonials . . . enthusiastic sharing . . . caring for the success of others . . . recognition, friendship, partnership and much more.

Christianity is a perfect example of the awesome power of Networking.

How Network Marketing Works

A Network Marketing company makes a product. Then they join in partnership with a network of independent distributors, each one in business for himself or herself. The company handles all the research and development, finance, management, public relations, warehousing, production, packaging, quality control, administration, shipping, data processing, and so on . . . and the company pays commission checks to all the distributors.

The distributors, in turn, market the products for the company.

As Charles Givens, financial expert and bestselling author of *Wealth Without Risk* points out, 80 percent of the cost of getting a product to consumers today is is the result of marketing expenses. That's why Network Marketing companies pay their distributors so well.

The company gives the distributors the support they need to market the products – brochures, flyers, tapes, etc. They even provide training in how to do the business.

The distributor's job is to move as much product as he or she can through an independent network of distributors – large or small – because distributors get paid on every product they sell. Since the individual distributors can sell only a small volume of products personally, they get other people to join them in the business as independent distributors. And the individual distributor gets a percentage of what these people sell as well.

And that's one of the powerful advantages Network Marketers and their companies have over more traditional, direct selling methods.

On the other hand, success in direct sales depends upon a few super salespeople who can each move a mountain of product. Network Marketing is just the opposite. Success in our business depends on *a lot of people doing a little bit each.* Believe me, it's a thousand times easier to teach people to accomplish that than it is to find and train super sales stars.

Network Marketers build a network of independent distributors, each of whom owns his or her own Network Marketing business selling products and building their own network of distributors. No matter when you join a network organization, you are always the head of your own company. Unlike conventional corporations with one chief executive at the top, in Network Marketing everyone is the CEO of his or her own independent organization. It's literally a network of CEOs.

Now, the Network Marketing company has done something pretty brilliant here. They've slashed a huge amount of money from their costs of distribution and sales. (Remember what Givens said – marketing accounts for 80% of a product's cost.) What they've created is a partnership with their distributors where the corporation provides everything they need – from product to promotional material – in exchange for the distributors' marketing efforts.

And the company gets rewarded, too – by reducing overhead and eliminating many of the conventional costs of doing business.

The company has no more need to pay for an in-house sales force – *and* they eliminate all the costs of the sales force's offices, support staff, phones, cars, travel and entertainment.

The company doesn't have to advertise anymore, either. The distributors do it for them with the most powerful advertising force of all time – word-of-mouth. Personal endorsements are the best way to educate and inform consumers about special products – which is the main reason you'll find some of the most unique, technically advanced, superior quality products in the world offered through Network Marketing.

The company doesn't employ – or pay for – jobbers, wholesalers, brokers, regional warehouses and store personnel – all those middlemen and middlewomen involved in retail distribution and sales who have their fingers in the profit pie. Since the company cut those jobs out, they've got all that money "left over" to pay the independent distributors who are moving the products.

It's simple – brilliantly simple.

There's no big mystery to Network Marketing. It's just another form of sales and distribution.

A new and better form? You be the judge.

Duplication – How Network Marketing Distributors Build Their Businesses

Have you ever heard of the doubling concept?

The word "duplicate" originally meant *to double,* and this concept of doubling is one of the most powerful forces at work in Network Marketing. Here's how it works:

If I offered you a million dollars cash, this very minute – or, if I offered to give you a penny doubled every day for a month... which would you choose?

If you're like most people, you'd probably choose the million dollars. But take my advice – don't do it. Take the penny doubled.

A penny doubled every day for a month doesn't sound like much, and it doesn't look like much in the beginning, either. After five days, you'd have all of 16 cents. After 15 days, you have a whopping $163.84.

Are you beginning to regret taking my advice? Hold on, there's more.

On day 19, you'd have $2,621. Six days later, day 25 – just 5 days before the end of the month – you'd have just over $167,000. The next day, $335,000. The next, more than $671,000. The next – the 28th day – you'd have over $1,340,000. And two days later, on the 30th – the last day of the month – you'd have a grand total of $5,368,709.12! That's over 5 million dollars!

All from one penny, which simply doubled every day.

This doubling principle is the way a business grows in Network Marketing.

You know, McDonalds didn't start off with 8,000 restaurants all over the world. They started with just one. And that's just how you can start in Network Marketing – you plus one other person.

Do you think it would be possible for you to find *just one person each month to join your business? Just one partner* who's interested in more freedom, recognition, happiness and security . . . one partner who's interested in improving the lives of his or her family?

One good person a month – that's all it takes!

And once you "sponsor" that person into the business with you, you become his or her coach – a teacher. You now don't need to concentrate all of your efforts on selling the products. You need to teach, to coach other people.

Now in month two, you teach your first new partner how to sponsor one person, while you sponsor another new person. So, at the end of month two, you've personally sponsored two people and your first partner has sponsored one as well. Now you've got a group of four – you and three others.

You do the same for month three, four, five and so on.

At then end of your first year, you'll have personally sponsored only 12 people – one each month. And each one of them has sponsored one person each month as well . . . and so on and so on. The true art of Networking, the awesome power of the doubling concept, is that by teaching each person how to sponsor and teach only one person a month, at the end of the year you would have 4,096 people in your organization!

Now, that's in a perfect world – and you know we don't live in a perfect world. Remember Murphy's Law: "Whatever can go wrong, will go wrong."

You know 80% of all businesses fail in the first year. So, let's say that 80 percent of your distributors are no longer selling products. These former sellers have now become consumers – so you're getting paid commissions on their reorders. Talk about a win/win situation!

Now let's take it one step further...let's assume the worst of the worst . . . let's assume 9 out of every 10 people you sponsor quits. To make matters worse, let's assume 90% of your entire group quits. Pretty bad news – don't you think? But look again – you still have 10% of your organization left . . . 10% of 4,096 people – that's over 400 people in your organization. And each one of them is bringing in new people and teaching them to do the business, just like you are.

Now, each one of these 400 people is using and selling products. Remember, that's how Network Marketers get paid – on the sales of products moved through their networks. So, if each person in your organization is moving $100 or $1000 worth of products per month, that's a total product volume of between $60,000 and $800,000 a month! Here comes the exciting part – the company pays the distributors a percentage of that sales volume.

If the Network Marketing company pays a five percent sales commission, that would be somewhere between $4000 to $40,000 *per month.*

Now you understand the power of Network Marketing!

Now, let's talk a little history.

Network Marketing Is 50 Years Young

In the early 1940s, a company called California Vitamins discovered that all their new sales reps were first satisfied customers – friends and family of their existing sales force. They also discovered that it was easier to get a lot of people who each sold a little product than it was to find those few superstars who could sell a whole lot all by themselves.

So, they combined those two ideas and designed a marketing and compensation structure that encouraged their sales people to recruit new distributors from the ranks of satisfied customers – most of whom were family and friends – and the company rewarded them for the sales their entire group produced. Even though each individual in the distributor network only sold a couple hundred dollars worth of products, the whole group moved tens of thousands of dollars worth of vitamins.

Network Marketing was born.

A few years later, the company changed its name to Nutralite. Two of its most successful distributors were Jay Van Andel and Rich DeVos. They went on to start their own Networking company – Amway. Today, as I told you, these gentlemen are two of the richest men in the world: they are numbers 10 and 11 on *Forbes* magazine's richest Americans list, each worth $2.9 billion – yes, *billion!*

Incidentally, the previous year *Forbes* listed them as numbers 50 and 51 . . . so they're also the fastest growing members on the rich list. And they started out as independent Network Marketing distributors.

Today, Network Marketing is going global, sweeping North America and the world.

Who's Involved in Network Marketing?

There are thousands of Network Marketing companies operating in the United States and Canada, Mexico, South America, the United Kingdom, Europe, Australia, New Zealand, Israel, Japan and the Pacific Basin. Little Malaysia alone has more than 800 active Network Marketing companies! In 1991, Amway was the fastest growing foreign company in Japan with sales of 700 million dollars – that ranks it with the likes of Mobil Oil and IBM! And in 1992, they predict 50,000 new distributors in Hungary!

In 1992, with the coming of the "United States of Europe," Network Marketing companies expect to explode in France, Germany, Italy and throughout Eastern Europe.

What kind of companies are involved in Network Marketing?

Network Marketing is reported to be a $40 billion industry, made up of Fortune 500 and New York Stock Exchange (NYSE) companies. Avon – the $3 billion cosmetic giant. Amway – at $3 billion plus in world-wide annual sales. Primerica – the Dow Jones insurance and financial services multi-national. And the list goes on – Shaklee, Tupperware, Fuller Brush, Rexall, Mary Kay Cosmetics.

Colgate-Palmolive and The Gillette Company have Network Marketing subsidiaries. In recent years U.S. Sprint and MCI generated more than 3,000,000 new customers for their long distance phone service. And a sizable number of those customers were taken from giant AT&T through – you guessed it – Network Marketing! How did AT&T respond to this "raid" on their customers? By contracting with several Network Marketing companies to move their long distance services! Hey, they didn't get to be a billion dollar company by being dumb!

The Companies and Their Products

Network Marketing companies have a 50-year history of innovation – and it shows in their product lines, which often feature leading-edge, hi-tech products. For example, Network Marketing companies also led the way with environmentally safe products with no additives and no preservatives . . . pesticide free, biodegradable products and packaging . . . and products made without animal testing – years before any of these became popular marketing trends.

In fact, Network Marketing companies have pioneered entire industries: natural vitamin and mineral supplements . . . nutrition and diet drinks . . . automotive engine additives and gas-saving devices... and concentrated, environmentally friendly household cleaners and detergents.

One Network Marketing company, National Safety Associates, almost single-handedly created the billion dollar home water filtration business. In the UK, one of the best selling – if not the top selling – fragrance lines is sold exclusively through Network Marketing.

Now that Network Marketing is gaining worldwide acceptance, more and more products are being offered through this dynamic industry every day. Today, you can buy at wholesale virtually any product you can find in a store – the variety of products and services is nearly endless. You can buy everything from groceries to automobiles . . . long-distance phone services to sports equipment . . . personal development seminars to discount travel services. In fact, one company offers over 5,000 products priced under $20!

What Kind of People Are Involved in Network Marketing?

People just like you and me. All kinds of people from every conceivable walk of life: Dr. Jay Clark, a dentist from New Mexico... Susan Fogg, a jazz dance teacher and mother of two... Bob Waller, a former bank president and founder... Stan Kingman, a baker... John Mann, a former cellist... Bo Batchelder, owner of a series of Taco Bell franchises... Rene Reid, who was once a nun and now is Chairperson of her County Commission's board... Eric Swan, a former stock broker... Sandy Elsberg, a former 1st grade teacher... and millions and millions of average North Americans, men and women from every state and province.

Here are the stories of a group of Network Marketers who represent a cross section of the kind of men and women involved in this business from the industry publication, *The Inside Report: Million Dollar Secrets From the Top Earners In Network Marketing.*

Dan and Paul Monayhan

Dan and Paul Monayhan are two young brothers. The older brother, Dan, had a bicycle-cart ice cream business that had just put him in debt $45,000. And Paul was a university student and part-time child care worker. Together, they built a Network Marketing business that in only 18 months climbed to an annual sales volume of $14 million!

One thing the brothers agree about is how Network Marketing is the most equal of all opportunities.

"It doesn't matter what your background is, " says Dan. "Not how old you are, where you're from, your family, education, successes or failures... nothing from your past matters at all. Network Marketing is for everybody – everybody who's willing to do what it takes to be a success."

"Our parents are in our Networking group, too," said Paul. "Our dad is a custodian and our mom's a part-time nurse. They came to see us – you know, they wanted to check out if this Network Marketing thing was okay for *their boys*. When they saw what we were doing, how easily it worked and how great the products were, they got involved, too. Now they make more money doing Network Marketing part-time than in their other jobs – and they love it!"

Jerome and Deborah Scott

"I enjoy working with people – always have," Jerome says. "Network Marketing is the perfect vehicle for achieving financial freedom, but it's more than that – it's freedom of *time*. It allows you to spend your time where you want to – with family and friends, pursuing the things in life that are really important to you.

"And of course, through leverage in Network Marketing, one can achieve phenomenal financial success. You may have heard the quote from J. Paul Getty, 'I'd much rather have one percent of 100 people's efforts than 100 percent of my own.' No matter how intelligent, energetic or dynamic you are – we all share the limitation of 24 hours to the day.

"You don't have the kinds of challenges in starting a Network Marketing business that you have in other businesses," Jerome adds. "It's not like franchising, where you need tens of thousands of dollars to get started. If you're a credible person and you've treated people well, and if you've got a strong product or service you want to share with people . . . then you're not going to have very many obstacles except those you place on yourself."

Jerome and Deborah Scott have earned over one million dollars in Network Marketing, and as Jerome says, their current earning level of $30,000 plus a month, "… buys a lot of quality time."

Jarman Massie

When you've been a professional dancer as well as professional tennis player, people are sure to know one thing about you – you're intent on making work and play one and the same thing. That's obviously so for Jarman Massie of Sausalito, California.

"There's one big key to my success in Network Marketing," says Jarman, "This business is in flow with my life. I don't do my life through the business. I do the business through my life.

"My success isn't all tied up in financial goals," Jarman says. "And I'm not saying the money isn't welcome – or useful. I'm saying that the money came as a result of living and working the way I wanted – not the other way around.

"Network Marketing has more opportunities to have fun and be with people who are having fun than any business or career, or anything at all, that I've ever done – and what's more, they pay me for it!" Jarman currently earns more than $12,500 per month in his Networking business. "I wouldn't dream of doing anything else," he says.

Dan Catto

Dan Catto, 36, once had a dream of owning his own small business. He was just 21 years old when he started at the bottom of the corporate ladder in a shoe company with retail outlets throughout Canada. In a few short years, he worked his way up to being the youngest general manager in the history of the company.

Then, the entrepreneurial bug bit him hard, and he left to start his own company. Within three years, his business – like 90 percent of all small business start-ups – was in bankruptcy. Dan turned back to the security of the corporate world, only to find himself looking for work again when his company was acquired by another, bigger one and his job was phased out. Heavily in debt, his marriage on the rocks, in ill health and stressed out to the edge of an emotional breakdown, Dan hit rock-bottom.

"It's amazing how open you become when there's no place else to go but up," Dan says. "When I was introduced to Network Marketing, I said, 'Sure – why not? I've got nothing *more* to lose. I've already lost everything anyway!'"

That was three and a half years ago. Today, Dan's living in a luxury condominium in downtown Toronto where a valet brings his new Jaguar around whenever he wants . . . and they pick up his laundry, too!

"I could retire today if I wanted," Dan said. "I already earn more money – and it's passive, residual income, too – than I've ever dreamed of earning!

"Probably more important than the money and the lifestyle," Dan says, "is the independence and freedom it's brought me. In any other business, the business ends up owning you. Not in Network Marketing. I can truly say that I own my own life. That's something very few people from any walk of life can say. And if I can do it – especially from where I started – anyone can do it, too. That's the beauty of Network Marketing. It's the greatest system of free enterprise in the world!"

Mary Magel

Mary Magel was the victim of the airline wars. The once prosperous carrier she had worked for as a flight attendant declared bankruptcy, leaving Mary without a job. At the same time, her husband's company transferred him from New York to Austin, Texas.

Mary looked for months for something to do where the skills she'd developed working with people could be used. She also wanted something she could do that would allow her to spend more time with her two children – something she'd come to cherish after leaving the airline industry. Then a friend of hers, also a former flight attendant, introduced her to Network Marketing.

"I was skeptical at first," said Mary, "but our friendship was strong, and besides I thought – if she can do it, I can do it. So, I gave it a try. After only six months in the business, I was making more part-time than my husband was in his full-time, corporate career!"

"I just got a monthly check for $25,000, and my husband went to the bank to deposit it for me," Mary said. "They held him up for half an hour, had a couple of bank officers come over – even the president of the bank – and check out the check. They'd never seen a paycheck that big and wanted to make sure it was real!

"I started off doubting this industry... doubting the money to be made... doubting myself." Mary said, "Now, I have no more doubts. Now I'm the one who makes believers out of skeptics!"

Melissa and Kim Anderson

Melissa Anderson is a C.P.A. who, after eight years in the auditing business, had come to hate her job. Kim was a former pro football player who loved his work, but knew it wouldn't last forever. So, after his football career, he became a police officer in Beverly Hills, California. But the Andersons wanted more, and turned to a part-time Network Marketing business.

"We were frightened at first – it was a little scary being so far out of our comfort zones." Melissa told us. "But, we wanted to do something together and we wanted to make some extra money, so we gave it a try.

"We earned more in our first month doing Network Marketing part-time than in our regular jobs combined," said Kim. "What's more, our day-to-day jobs were so boring compared to working with the people we met in our Networking business.

"When we first started in Network Marketing, we had a dream-goal of earning $60,000 a year. That's changed, too. We're right on the verge of making five figures a month – and there's no telling how far we can go. The freedom, the lifestyle – it's all great. It's a blessing.

"At one time, all we could think about was ourselves," Melissa said, "You know, paying the bills, how we could get by, that kind of thing. Now, we're doing what we *want* to do. We're traveling, enjoying people, investing our money better, helping different church ministries, really helping others. Like we said, Network Marketing is a blessing."

Jan D'Agostino

Ask Jan D'Agostino why she's involved in Network Marketing, and she's quick to answer, "Because it's the greatest opportunity in the history of the world!" And she goes on to say, "I'm involved in Network Marketing because I didn't have to go to college and get a degree to have the income I'm having now. And, it's a no-risk business. It sure beats the $55,000 I had to invest in my beauty salon just to open the doors! What's more, it's fun."

Jan's been involved with her own home-based business for a little over two and a half years now. She works full-time in Network Marketing and earns over $100,000 annually.

"Network Marketing allows me to be who I am – in my heart *and* in my business. That's something I've never found anywhere else, and I wouldn't trade it for the world!"

Kathy Brown

When Kathy first heard about Network Marketing, she was an intensive care nurse, the active mother of four children, and she taught aerobics at a local health spa.

"When a friend first told me about Network Marketing, I was too busy to listen," Kathy says. "Besides, the truth was, I was turned off. I was skeptical about all of it. I don't know why I took a look at it, but I did – and *I'm glad I did!*"

Just one short year after getting into Network Marketing, Kathy has distributors in all 50 states, as well as in England and Germany. Kathy earns well over $100,000 annually and has had a number of super months where her net income topped $19,000!

"I've got doctors, lawyers, professionals and people from all walks of life in my business," Kathy told us. "There's no question in my mind – the longer I'm involved, the more I see where this whole industry is going. Network Marketing is definitely the way to distribute products in the 90s!

"What's so great about this business," Kathy adds, "is that you are in business for yourself – but *not* by yourself.

"Network Marketing has been absolutely life-altering for me. I thank God for the opportunity to do Network Marketing. I love it!"

Rudolf Molnar

Rudolf Molnar escaped from Romania with his wife, Anna, and young son 17 years ago. He arrived in America as so many had before him – penniless. He knew no one, and what little English he knew hardly got him a bite to eat. But Rudolf shared the dream of so many immigrants: in America, anyone who worked hard enough and smart enough could become a millionaire.

Over the years, Rudolf held a number of jobs. He settled into a career of being the superintendent and rental agent for an apartment building. Hardly the fast track to a million dollars.

Then, Rudolf discovered Network Marketing. It took him three years to achieve his dream. Rudolf Molnar is now a millionaire!

"This is only possible in the U.S.A.," Rudolf says. "I know why it's called the land of opportunity. And there's no better way for average people to earn above average income than Network Marketing.

"I was in a communist country. I hated being controlled. In Network Marketing, *you* are in control.

You tell *you* what to do. That's freedom. That's America. That's Network Marketing.

"We own a beautiful home on an island in Siesta Key, Florida, and I go fishing in my boat whenever I want. We own a Mercedes and a bunch of other cars. We travel around the country and the world. My son's in college, and when he gets out, he'll come into the business, too. None of this would be possible without Network Marketing. We're very lucky."

Terry Hill

Terry Hill was considered *extremely* successful. She was one of the leading sales representatives for Xerox – one of the top ten sales people in the nation every year. But she was paying too high a price.

"I found out that to be successful in corporate America, you have to be obsessed, possessed, totally 100 percent committed and married to that career," Terry says."… and I was. That's why I did so well year after year – I committed myself totally to Xerox and made it my number one priority."

But the down side was getting Terry down. "After being in that industry for almost ten years, I had no life outside of Xerox. I was entering my 30s and thought, 'I don't want to be a single woman, in my 40s or 50s, with no family and no personal life. There's got to be more to this than just making money and being successful.' It's a very empty feeling.

"I'd wanted that achievement very badly," Terry added, "but now that I'd reached it, it was time to move on. I wanted something more fulfilling – but I didn't want to give up the kind of lifestyle to which I had become accustomed."

That was four years ago. Today, Terry Hill has earned more than a million dollars in Network Marketing and currently makes more than $25,000 per month. She and her husband, Tom (who left a success-ful career as a broker with Merrill Lynch) work together in their Networking business.

"This is the best of all times to get involved with Network Marketing," Terry says, "because it's still somewhat new and fresh, yet it's got credibility. It's been around long enough that it's not something that people think just came from outer space. It's become a believable opportunity. It's gained a lot of respect in the last few years, but it's still a *very* new industry, as far as how many people in North America are doing it and truly know about it.

"More and more companies in America are going to it. Companies – like Xerox – are wanting to know how they can market things through Network Marketing. It's a win-win situation for people. And I think in the '90s, people are going to be sick and tired of backbiting and greed and competition in the marketplace . . . and tired of not being able to trust . . . and tired of being stuck in such an impersonalized, uncaring career life. And Network Marketing is an answer to all those things – and more."

Cooperation Versus Competition

One of the big reasons for the success of Network Marketing in the 1990s is that it is based on coopera-tion – *not* competition. Unlike traditional business, career advancement in Network Marketing comes directly from your helping to create success for all the people in your group, in your company and in the industry as a whole.

It's much like the story of the woman who died and suddenly found herself at St. Peter's door. She asked him to show her the difference between Heaven and Hell.

St. Peter took her to Hell where she saw an endless banquet table set with the most abundant spread of magnificent, mouth-watering food and drink she'd ever seen! Yet the people seated at the table were all shrieking and crying, wailing and pulling at their hair and tearing their clothes to rags. She had never seen such horrible pain and anguish.

She was about to ask St. Peter why – in the face of such delicious abundance – the people were so miserable. But as she glanced around, she discovered the answer for herself. All their eating utensils were three feet long! None of the people at the table could even get a taste of the luscious feast.

When she arrived in Heaven, she was surprised to find the exact same scene: the same endless table, the same fantastic food and drink – even the same three-foot long forks and spoons. But here, everybody was happy and laughing, having a wonderful time. "Why are they happy here?", she wondered out loud.

"Because," St. Peter whispered, "in Heaven, the people reach across the table and feed each other."

Cooperation instead of competition is a powerful reason that more and more people are attracted to the Network Marketing concept every day.

Why Are People Involved in Network Marketing?

They're involved because they have a burning desire for a better way to live and work.

They're involved because they dared to dream their dreams could come true.

They're involved because they had the guts to get off their butts and do something to change their circumstances for the better.

They're involved because they're passionate about being paid what they're really worth.

They're involved because somebody cared enough about them to show them the awesome opportunity of Network Marketing.

And they're involved because they were *ready* to make a change.

Folks, here's the truth: Network Marketing *is* in your future. One way or the other you *will* be involved. How you are involved is up to you – nobody else. You're either going to be spending money, buying products – and lots of them – from Network Marketers. Or you're going to be selling products and building an organization – and making money. It's your choice.

Ask yourself, "Would I rather be the one spending the money . . . or the one making the money?"

Friends, we can't live on two incomes today the way our parents did on one! It's a new world. Remember, less than one half of one percent of all North Americans earn $100,000 a year or more. And if you want to be one of them, you're going to have to do something new and different.

Network Marketing – The New Way to Financial Freedom

You'll never create real and lasting wealth trading time for money. Even the doctors, lawyers and Indian chiefs can't do it anymore – and if the high priced college kids can't cut it, how can you?

In Network Marketing you can break out of the time-for-money trap.

Passive income... residual income is where it's at. How many self-employed people do you know who can take off for a month and come back to a bigger paycheck than when they left? In fact, how many can come back and find their business in one piece?

In Network Marketing you could do just that. I've known a number of Network Marketers who left for a honeymoon or an extended vacation . . . and returned to find an even bigger check waiting for them than when they left! That's the power of passive income!

If you're a woman . . . if you're black, hispanic or any other minority . . . or if you're one of those people *without* a specialized, professional university degree – both the corporate world and the professional world are generally closed to you.

Not Network Marketing – it's wide open. No glass ceiling – no any-kind-of ceiling. You're free.

Look, I'm no different than you. I'm no smarter. I went to college and didn't learn how to become financially independent. I've had jobs, people telling me what to do... punching a clock... fighting traffic... the rat race. I was making $5.50 an hour building boats. I waited on tables – gettin' nowhere in a hurry. I've had my own business, too. I got out just in time and only lost close to a quarter of a million dollars!

But I made a fortune because of Network Marketing. Will you?

If you're willing to work... if you're teachable... and if you have a burning desire to become successful, then yes – you can make it in Network Marketing.

Johnny Carson once said:

"Talent alone won't make you a success. Neither will being at the right place at the right time, unless you are ready. The most important question is: 'Are you ready?' "

Right here – right now *is* the right time and the right place for Network Marketing.

It's interesting how resistant we are to change. Even when the handwriting is all over the wall, we want to stay in our comfort zones – even when we're the most uncomfortable . . . even when we're miserable.

Let's not sugar-coat it. For things to change, you have to change. For things to get better, you have to get better.

You can curse your parents, your boss, the government and whatever. But one simple fact remains: when it becomes harder to suffer than change, you will change.

Like the Chinese say, "If you don't change your direction – you're bound to end up where you're headed."

■ ■ ■

CHAPTER TWELVE

If Network Marketing Is So Great – Why Haven't We Been Told the Truth about It?

*"Before us lie two paths – honesty and dishonesty.
The shortsighted embark on the dishonest path;
the wise on the honest. For the wise know the truth:
in helping others we help ourselves; and in hurting
others we hurt ourselves.... Honesty is still the best policy."*
                              - ***Wynn Davis,*** *"The Best of Success"*

Why haven't we been told the truth about Network Marketing?

Because the world is filled with not-so-wise, dishonest people – shortsighted men and women who have yet to discover that in hurting others, they hurt themselves most of all. Remember Carlo Ponzi – the inventor of the pyramid scheme?

Remember the subtitle of this book?

"The book your boss doesn't want you to read."

Why would I say that?

Because it's not in your boss' interest for you to learn there's a new and better way to live and work – a way that doesn't include the 9 to 5, trading time for money insecurity trap of having someone else own your life... someone in command of the two words that stand between you and the street – "you're fired!"

There are lots of "someone elses" out there – lots of them! And it's not just your "boss" at work I'm talking about. It's *all* the self-proclaimed "bosses" in government, education, business, etc., who think *they* know what's best for you and me. How do they know?

Power to the People

The truth is that most of the people in power today are scared to death. Their overriding concern is the fear of loss – loss of their own power! Everywhere they turn, they see the handwriting on the wall – and they don't like the message. So what do they do? They shoot the messenger.

Well, Network Marketing's message is "power to the people" – not just the "bosses."

We've come a long way since the 1960s. Remember the anti-establishment movement? How so many of us wanted to change the way the world worked? Well, one reason that "revolution" *didn't* work was because we didn't have a new and better way of doing things to replace the old paradigm.

Now we do. That's why more and more Network Marketing companies are wearing bullet-proof vests.

Remember how the Romans treated the Christians? They fed them to the lions!

Remember what the power-people did with franchising in the beginning? They called it a scam and a scheme. They were threatened by the message, so they tried to shoot the messenger full of holes.

The media powers searched for all the dirty stories they could find. Blew them up bigger than life and tried to take franchising down. Why?

Because they were already kings of the mountain, doing business with the other corporate kings – and these upstart franchises were saying, "The hell with you. We're going to make our own mountain!" And they did!

Money Is Serious Business

How many millions of dollars of advertising space do you think those first franchise firms were buying – versus all the advertising bought by the traditional manufacturers and their conventional retail outlets that the franchises threatened with their new and better way?

Newspapers, magazines, radio and television do *not* make a profit on readers, subscribers, listeners and viewers. The media make money from their advertisers. BIG money. Outrageous money! And if you're not one of them – one of those big ticket advertisers – you don't get the positive press coverage you need, much less deserve. Why should you? You're not making the media any money.

What's more – what if you're some upstart competitive marketer taking sales and profits away from those big ticket advertisers?

Do you really think Howard Johnson's was thrilled to death at Ray Kroc and his McDonalds? Once McDonalds got big enough to start taking market share away from those guys – and all the other established restaurants that advertised heavily in newspapers, radio and T.V. . . . . it was war! And whose side was the media on?

Hey, even Fortune 500 companies who owned and invested in the franchise concept were afraid of telling the public the truth that *they* were involved. Play it safe. "If this thing goes bust – nobody will know *we* blew it."

Courage, guys.

- Retailers put the pressure on....
  (They were losing sales)

- Manufacturers put the pressure on....
  (So were they)

- The media put the pressure on.... *(Their advertisers were being hurt – and the new guys weren't spending anywhere near what the good old boys were spending in advertising)*

- Even the politicians – lobbied by big payroll employers with big blocks of votes and even bigger campaign contributions – put the pressure on. They tried to pass laws against it. They said franchising should be illegal!

It's a wonder franchising survived.

But it did survive – and it prospered because it was a new and better way of doing things . . .and because what you resist – persists. Over one-third of *everything* we buy today comes from a franchise – Taco Bell, The Gap, Mrs. Field's Cookies, Jazzercise, Century 21, etc., etc., etc. – $758.5 billion dollars worth!!!

Do you see any more nasty newspaper articles today on franchising? Any more exposés on 20/20? "You deserve a break today...." "Where's the Beef?" Advertising has burned the slogans of big franchises into our cultural consciousness..

Can you name one industry that does more advertising today – in newspapers, magazines, radio and TV – than franchising?

And with all the money the franchising industry makes ... and with the tremendous number of people employed by franchises across North America ... and with the awesome contribution franchises make to federal, state and local economies . . . and with the taxes they generate and all the *votes* they buy... how happy and cooperative are the politicians and media about the franchise industry now?

Folks, money talks . . . and you know what walks.

Mugging the Competition

That's the way the game is played. If you wanta' play with the big boys, you better be one of them. If you're not, they'll crush you like a bug hitting the windshield at 60 miles per hour.

Just look at how one giant corporation, a recognized leader in the $15 billion-a-year commercial indoor air filtration industry, handled some serious competition from an upstart Network Marketing company.

The giant put in a bid to clean up the air in a carpet warehouse – to the tune of one million plus dollars! A little local Network Marketing company called Alpine Air Products bid for the same job . . . for a little over $100,000. You guessed it . . . the little guy got the contract.

Now I ask you, how do you think big Goliath felt about little David eating his lunch? What would you do if you were heading up the sales' team that lost a major contract to one of those "pyramid" companies? Would you cry in your beer and curse your luck? Or would you call out the dogs of war?

A few days later the media pollution hit the fan when a local T.V. station aired an "expose" claiming that Alpine's machines poisoned the air instead of purifying it – which was totally ridiculous! The State Attorney General got in on the act, too, and filed a lawsuit against Alpine. Alpine ended up losing the contract – and they almost lost everything.

There's a happy ending, however. Like we've told you again and again, if you've got a new and better way, it will eventually triumph in a free market. Today Alpine is doing more business than ever. And the giant? They're laying off workers by the thousands (and they're still losing bids to Alpine).

Let's face it. Stories like this are the reason you haven't been told the truth about Network Marketing.

And it's getting worse now because we're getting too big for our britches.

And that's even harder for the "giants" to take because they've got the sneaking suspicion we just may be right....

We may really be the wave of the future....

We may really have managed to put the freedom they stole back into free enterprise.

After all, there are thousands of Network Marketers . . . and millions of satisfied customers world-wide . . . and billions of dollars worth of products sold every year through Network Marketing!

Bigger Is *Not* Always Better

Recently, a Network Marketing company that sold personal care products, NuSkin International, took it square on the chin from the media and several State Attorney Generals (AGs)! This "little" Networking company was becoming not-so-little anymore. They were projecting annual 1991 sales in the neighborhood of $500 million dollars– that's half a billion dollars!

Now, where were all those sales coming from?

They were *not* coming from men and women who had never bought skin care products before.

Those sales were being taken away from the big guys – Revlon, Max Factor, Estee Lauder and other big cosmetic and health and beauty aids manufacturers.

How do you think the big boys felt about that? Do you think they were pleased with the success of the new kid on the block?

They were pleased all right – they were shaking in their shoes!

Do you know what *really* bugged Revlon and the rest? These new Networking kids were *not* spending multi-millions of dollars on monster advertising budgets in magazines and on T.V. like *they* were forced to

And since NuSkin was a Network Marketing company, it didn't pour *all* its cash down the throats of middlemen, wholesalers, brokers, jobbers, and retailers – expensive distributors who drive up the price of the products without adding any value at all. Instead the companies were putting this money into the pockets of people like you and me.

Furthermore, the big guys weren't bypassing the department stores and malls – like the Network Marketing company was – going right into the consumer's living room with person-to-person education, information, sharing-caring service and time-saving convenience.

Not to mention the fact that this "little" Network

Marketing company had a dedicated, growing sales force of 100,000 independent distributors nationwide who owned their own, mostly part-time, Networking businesses... and these distributors were being paid to say nice things about the products (has any company ever paid you for doing that?)... and a whole bunch of them were making real good money... and a few of them were even getting filthy rich, making upwards of $250,000 *per month!!!*

The Economics of Competition

Now, if you were sitting around the conference room in one of those big companies and your sales were slipping away – being *stolen* from you by an upstart, punk Network Marketing company *that you simply could not compete with* – what would you do?

Or if you were one of the brokers, retailers, wholesalers, media people, truckers, or any of the other people whose jobs or businesses were being threatened with extinction because Network Marketing was a new and better way of doing things – what would you do?

Well, if you had a friend in the State Attorney General's office – you'd make a call, wouldn't you? And if you had an industry lobbyist or political action group that you had been contributing a bunch of money to, you'd call them too, wouldn't you?

In fact, if your job was on the line – either as the VP of sales or one of the executive staff who sooner-or-later had to answer to stockholders and explain why your market share was being taken away by some stupid little "pyramid scheme" – you'd grab any strategy you could get your hands on and fight back – wouldn't you?

Remember, your future's at stake here... your position, your power – *your paycheck!*

Look, as I told you earlier, I'm not here to champion any particular Network Marketing company. My commitment is to the industry . . . and to you! But I'll guarantee you this – I'm damn sure not going to stand around with my hands in my pockets and let the bullies take over the beach!

The Economics of Politics

Don't you find it odd that the state AG who made the most noise recently about NuSkin – the little $500,000,000 a year personal care products company – whose regulatory problems were written up in *USA Today, Newsweek,* etc., etc. – was from Michigan...? He didn't risk very many Michigan votes by picking on a company that employed lots of people and paid a bundle of local and state taxes in far-off Utah.

He was coming into an election year! And there's nothing like a big Law 'n' Order bust of an out-of-state company to get your name plastered all over the front page . . . a company with very few Michigan voters to cause a political backlash. This guy was on a roll – and there was nobody to stop him.

He even made it on national T.V. He was on ABC – Ted Koppel's *Nightline* – as an expert on the legal side of the Network Marketing business. Sadly, Ted was indisposed and Barbara Walters sat in. And boy was she ever unprepared! I was embarrassed for her!

At one point in the broadcast, the Attorney General from Michigan is explaining why – in terms of "the law" – that NuSkin was an "illegal pyramid scheme." And he holds up a graph of their compensation plan from a page in the company's training manual and says, "Look, it's even shaped like a pyramid."

Is that an idiotic statement or what? This guy's head must be shaped like a pyramid...and his brain's at the top!

And to think this guy is an Attorney General running for re-election. No wonder there are so many "Throw The Bums Out" bumper stickers during this election year!

The Media Pulls the Strings

And oh – Barbara Walters! What do you suppose she would have said, what probing and provocative questions would she have asked if that Network Marketing company were a $5 million a year advertiser with a bunch of 30-second spots on ABC's 20/20? When was the last time you saw an expose on a company that spends millions every year on T.V. advertising . . . like McDonalds? Or Pepsi? Or Nike? Never! Do you know why? Ever hear the expression, "Don't bite the hand that feeds you"?

If Network Marketing were helping to pay Barbara's salary, I'll bet "the show would go on" a little differently.

When *USA Today* published its story on the whole affair, do you know what happened next? NuSkin,the company under fire, was forced to take out a couple of full page ads to explain its side of the story. Those pages run $60,000 plus a pop. Any connection?

Listen, there were lots of smaller Network Marketing companies catching flack from some state's AG. But don't bother picking on them – they can't afford to counter with a couple of hundred thousand dollars worth of ads. Why bother with them. Go for the *big* story – especially if there's *big* money there for the taking.

This particular "little" Network Marketing company had pretty deep pockets – and they all knew it!

It's happened before. The regulators nailed Amway back in the 70s for the same reason. Herbalife – who had reached $500 million in sales – was almost destroyed a number of years ago. And the same thing has happened again and again to a number of Network Marketing companies.

Does this scenerio sound familiar to what happened to franchising in the 60's? But just look at franchising today!

Do Your Homework

Now, let's get one thing straight. Just as there are scams and schemes in any industry, there are a few Network Marketing companies that are blatantly illegal. There are good and bad apples in every industry, aren't there? Real estate has it's swampland scams . . . banking has it's savings and loan crooks . . . the stock market has it's insider trading scandals . . . and so on. So why should Network Marketing be any different?

It's a fact of life today that you can't be too trusting or naive. So open your eyes and ears. Check out the product . . . the people . . . the company . . . everything!

Be careful. And know what you're getting into. That's good advice whether you're walking down a dark street . . . investing in the stock market . . . or getting started in a new business.

Another Thing about "Advertising":

Years ago, John Wanamaker said:

"50 percent of my advertising is wasted – I just don't know which half!"

Today the advertising industry is on the ropes. The current struggling economy is killing them. So, you tell me, is it in the media's interest to say anything positive about the Network Marketing industry? Especially at a time when they're desperate for advertising dollars!

Let's face facts – the media has no love for an industry that doesn't have any major advertising bills to pay . . . and never will!

Negative Motivation

Is there a positive side to this flood of negativity the media dumps on Network Marketing? You bet – although I've got to say, I'll be one of the first to rejoice when they begin to praise us instead of trying to cut us down. But let me illustrate the good news resulting from all the bad news with a story.

One day there were two curious frogs who fell into a pail of milk. Now the pail was pretty deep, so it was a long way up to get out of the pail. The frogs started jumping and jumping, but neither of them could quite reach the top edge of the pail.

It just so happened that one of the frogs was nearly deaf. So he didn't particularly notice at first that a number of frogs had gathered at the rim of the pail and were razzin' and jeerin' at him and his friend. They laughed and pointed at the two stuck in the pail. They mocked them and called them names.

Now the other frog heard all of this and he became pretty angry. He jumped and jumped, just saying to himself, "I'll show those guys – wait til' I get my hands on them." But after a while, he got tired. He became dejected and bitter, and the more the frogs outside taunted him, the more depressed he became. Finally, he gave up hope, stopped trying to jump out and drowned.

The other frog – the one who was a nearly deaf – didn't hear the negativity of his buddies and he kept trying and trying. Every time he looked up at them, he got even more determined and would jump even higher. Eventually, all of his jumping around turned the milk to butter – and he was able to jump free of the pail with one easy hop.

When he got out, the other frogs asked him why all their name calling and making fun of him hadn't discouraged him like the other frog. The frog replied, "Gee, I had no idea you were puttin' me down. I thought you were cheering me on!"

There are many "hard-of-hearing frogs" in Network Marketing today.

We think Barbara Walters is just cheering us on.

"You Have the Right to..." Except in Network Marketing

What's the very first amendment to the Bill of Rights of the Constitution of the United States of America?

And I quote:

"Congress shall make no law... abridging the freedom of speech...."

Well, I guess a number of states and the Federal Trade Commission (FTC) can "abridge" anyway. I guess the Constitution doesn't apply to them.

You see, you – whoever you are, whatever you do for a living – can stand up any time, any where ... in front of any number of people ... and tell them how much income you earn – *unless* you are a Network Marketer.

Check this out. In some states, Network Marketers are not permitted to mention their incomes in public.

I suppose they are allowed to lock themselves in the bathroom and scream out the numbers on their most recent commission checks until they turn blue. But they cannot tell a group of people. If they do, the state Attorney Generals will invite them to jail and the FTC will – if the numbers are big enough to make it worth their while – swoop down on them like starving legal eagles.

I know a Network Marketer named Mark. Mark's a high-profile guy, one of the top income earners with his company.

Mark has earned as much as $250,000 a month from his Network Marketing business (not bad for a former minister who was an inch away from having his car repossessed five years ago). Today he doesn't dare tell anyone how much he makes. But he has been investigated by the FTC and a couple of state regulators, anyway. Why? Simply because he makes such an outrageous amount of money – that's why!

Mark finds it absolutely amazing that he cannot say how much money he makes! Is this our constitutional right of freedom of speech in action?

What the Attorney Generals say Mark and the rest of us in this business *can* do is to take all the money your company paid out in commissions in your local geographic region, divide it by the total number of distributors in that area – both active ones and those who aren't even involved anymore – and you can tell everybody *that* figure.

It's like forcing a professional athlete like Joe Montana to state his income only in terms of the average salary of all the San Francisco 49ers put together ... including all the retired players! Can you imagine that?

I mean, pick any profession – lawyers, doctors, actors, writers – are they forced to do that? Does the government single them out for a special dose of unconstitutional "abridging the freedom of speech...." They wouldn't stand for it. Neither would you.

But for Network Marketers, that's the way it is.

In a recent issue of *SUCCESS* magazine, successful Network Marketer Terry Hill (who you'll remember was one of the top ten sales reps for Xerox for ten years running), explained it this way:

"When I interviewed for a job with Xerox, I asked them, 'What's the most money I could make?' And they told me I never would have gone to work for them if they hadn't. But suppose they were required by law to tell you only what the lowest paid person on the staff makes. That's what I have to do when I introduce people to Network Marketing business – that's ridiculous!

Network Marketing Money Is Just too Much!

A couple of years ago, *U.S. News and World Report* published a list of the highest income earning occupations in America. They listed the specific career and gave the upper income earning range.

They omitted the income for Network Marketers. They said it wasn't believable!

Now *that's* unbelievable!

I guess it's true what they say about how the more powerful you are, the bigger your enemies are, too.

Tell me, if you were sitting atop the Prudential building in Boston and the talk around the big polished conference table was about how come you're not selling more life insurance. And let's say some junior executive (clearly on his way *down*) had the stupidity to say that A. L. Williams (a Network Marketing company now owned by Primerica – one of the Dow Jones 30 industrials) wrote more individual life coverage than "The Pru," the biggest insurance company in the world – what would you think? What would you do?

If you were involved with any of these major companies whose lunch was getting eaten slowly but surely by an upstart industry . . . an industry that talks to consumers face to face – what would you do?

Remember the rule: "If you can't beat 'em – join 'em"?

Well, these traditional companies have their own rule: "If you can't beat 'em – beat 'em up!"

Is There Anybody Who *Isn't* Trying to Beat-up on Network Marketing?

Sure. Sprint and MCI are two. They both offer long-distance phone service at "discount" rates.

Together they stole *three million* customers away from AT&T, many of them through Network Marketing. They're very happy campers.

And you know who else isn't trying to beat up on Network Marketing anymore?

AT&T. Although they don't say so publicly (remember all those Fortune 500 companies who were into franchising but played it safe and wouldn't admit it at first) . . . Ol' Ma' Bell has been pursuing relationships with Network Marketing companies for a few years now. Why? They've felt its power right where it matters most – in the wallet – and they're jumping on board.

Avon – the $3 billion cosmetics giant – was having trouble keeping their sales people. You know how they're solving the problem? Shifting their emphasis from direct sales to Network Marketing!

You've heard of the Fuller Brush Company. They've been in direct sales for more than 80 years. Our grandmothers bought whisk brooms from them. Now, they're moving completely over to Network Marketing.

General Motors sells cars through Network Marketing. Rexall (the national drug store chain) now has a Network Marketing division. They're testing the marketing waters to see if it's profitable to sell a number of their own house-brand products through our "new and better"methods.

More and more corporations have stopped trying to beat us – and started joining us.

Why? Because Network Marketing is making more and more common sense – which in business is defined as dollars and cents – the bottom line.

Meanwhile, costs in the conventional marketing world have gone crazy:

- Advertising is too expensive even for multi-million dollar companies....

- Distribution and sales costs are skyrocketing....

- Thousands of wonderful products that consumers really want never make it to the marketplace because even the biggest companies simply cannot afford the high cost of marketing their products . . .

- Consumers no longer trust companies or their ads, and retail clerks don't know their left hand from their right as to how to educate and inform shoppers about what they're buying or how to use it....

- Consumers are demanding more for their money.

- Consumers are demanding better customer service and shop-at-home convenience.....

- And competition is getting tougher and tougher *and* tougher *for everyone...*

The unconventional approach of Network Marketing has more and more of the right answers – right when business needs them most.

I know you haven't been told the truth about Network Marketing before.

Now, you've got a pretty good idea why.

And you know what? In a way, I'm kinda' glad we haven't been told the truth.

Network Marketing Is Still a Best-Kept Secret

It's like finding a great fishing hole. The kind where you throw your line in and – bang! – catch fish in minutes. Then another and another. Big ones, too! It's the kind of discovery you share carefully. It's a secret. You only tell your good friends about it.

Network Marketing is like the gold mine story about a man who was driving along a mountain road late at night when his headlights reflected off something bright on the side of the road.

The man eased his truck onto the shoulder, grabbed his flashlight and walked over to the bushes where he thought he saw the object.

He parted the bushes and scanned the ground with his flashlight. As he pushed back the final branch, he was astonished to find himself staring at a bar of gold near the opening to a huge cave. He lunged forward and explored the cave with his flashlight. It was filled with gold bars!

The man couldn't believe his good fortune! He grabbed an armful of gold bars and loaded up his truck. But when he came back to the cave, he was even more amazed . . . magically, there were twice as many gold bars than there were before!

He worked fast and furious and filled his truck so full of gold bars that the tires were ready to burst. By the time he left, the gold bars were spilling out of the cave, through the bushes and even closer to the road. He covered the opening to the cave with the bushes as best he could and headed for home.

Now let me ask you. If you were that man, who would you share your gold mine secret with? Would you run an ad in the local newspaper or stop strangers on the street and tell them you had discovered a gold mine? Or would you share your discovery with people you know and care about? Of course you'd tell those people closest to you first, wouldn't you?

I admit it – there's a part of me that thinks Network Marketing is like a gold mine. I mean, I like the idea that average people are turning their lives around – ordinary people living extraordinary lives. It's really okay with me if the big boys come to the party – sooner or later. But truthfully, I'm real content to make it later. Much later. Make 'em wait and sweat for it. After all, that's what they've been doing to you and me *for years*.

I know they're coming. Everybody is. It's just a matter of time. But before they do, before Network Marketing gets to be a multi-hundred-billion dollar industry like franchising, I want us all to get ours.

The people who had The American Dream stolen from them should have the first shot. I'm up for letting the old paradigm thieves get the crumbs this time.

What's the song say:

"And the first one now – Will later be last – For the times they are a-changin'."

Folks, "The answer *is* blowin' in the wind."
It's going to be the biggest hurricane in history.
And its name is Network Marketing.

■ ■ ■

Phase Five:

Network Marketing and YOU

■

CHAPTER THIRTEEN

Why Is Network Marketing Exploding?

Throughout this book, we've pointed out how times have changed and how they'll be changing even faster tomorrow. We've pointed out how technology is marching – more correctly *racing* – forward, making entire industries and ways of working obsolete almost overnight.

It's because of technology that Network Marketing is exploding!

Before the computer, no Network Marketing company could grow any bigger than their ability to keep track of their distributors. Imagine having to take and process orders, keep track of individual network organizations and issue timely and accurate commission checks for 10 or 20 thousand distributors. Impossible! Not anymore, thanks to computer technology.

It's hard to imagine Network Marketing without credit cards, airplanes that go coast to coast in less than six hours, discount long distance telephone service, copying machines, 800 phone numbers, etc.

Network Marketers today can FAX product and training information anywhere in the world in an instant. They can prospect for new partners on their car phones – while stuck in traffic. A thousand people or more can get on a weekly teleconference call and invite new people to hear all about the company's products and opportunity, without leaving their own living rooms!

Today Network Marketers can tell people across the country (or around the world, for that matter) about their company, products and income opportunity by sending them an audio or video tape. They could even train their new long-distance partners with tapes. Talk about convenience – for just a few dollars you could send your new distributors the best training seminars presented by the best trainers in the business!

None of this was possible 20 years ago. Much of it wasn't available or affordable even five years ago. Car phones, copying machines, teleconferences, voice mail, videos, audio cassettes, home computers . . . And tomorrow's technology is even more extraordinary.

Imagine selecting the Network Marketing products you want from a full-color talking catalog on your home computer in the kitchen . . . imagine ordering what you want simply by touching the screen... imagine having telephone calls and conferences while looking at the people you're talking to (this one's here today – AT&T just introduced their video phone!)... imagine having multi-media video presentations sent directly to your home by satellite whenever you want . . imagine talking back to your computer or TV with interactive programming . . . imagine having your monthly commission checks automatically and instantly transferred to your electronic checking account....

The extraordinary advance of technology is opening up vast horizons of possibility for Network Marketing – and it's happening right now. That's why Network Marketing is just coming into its own.

Hard Times – Tough Choices

We've talked about the reality of the most productive time in this nation's history, yet a time when tens of millions of people will be without work, a time of 20 percent unemployment!

We've talked about The American Dream of health, happiness, security and freedom . . .and how fewer and fewer people are in a position to have even one or two of these qualities in their lives, much less all of them.

We've talked about how the odds are stacked against us in the working world today . . .about glass ceilings, "unequal opportunity," the sand trap of using a college education to lead to a corporate career track and the scams and schemes that rip off almost any chance we have for getting to the top and living the good life.

We've talked about the lack of real creativity and control in the work place. . . and the lack of satisfaction and fulfillment available in most conventional jobs.

We've discussed illegal and legal pyramid schemes and how they're sucking the life out of the average American woman and man.

We've talked about how frustrated people are . . . how angry people are at what's happening . . . and how millions of people are feeling totally powerless to do anything about it.

What we've shown – sadly – is that for most of us, the future can be a pretty hopeless situation.

Remember the definition of hope that said, "Hope was the expectation that someone, or something, would come along and save your butt."

My friends, *no one* and *no thing* is going to come along and save your anything. Sure, you may hit the lottery. But it's pretty hopeless when all that's left of The American Dream is a zillion-in-one chance to make it big.

Let me tell you a wonderful story.

Dreaming of Success

One day, a man came into a psychiatrist's office and boy, did he look bad! He was ashen gray – like death warmed over – and he was shaking all over, too. His eyes were sunk deep into his head, dark circles under the circles under his eyes. He hadn't slept in months! He begged the doctor to help him!

The man told the psychiatrist about a recurring dream he'd been having:

Every time he'd fall asleep he'd have the same frightening nightmare. There he was, just walking down the street. He'd go right up to this building… up to this huge door, and no matter what he did – he could never get inside!

He'd push and strain against the door – nothing! It wouldn't budge an inch. No matter how hard he struggled, no matter what near superhuman strength he could muster – nothing. He couldn't get in!

He would wake up in a cold sweat, shaking – scared and exhausted. It was so bad, no matter how tired he became, he was afraid to close his eyes. He said it felt like he was going to die if he didn't get in – and he couldn't!

The doctor asked him why it was so important to open that door, and the man replied that it was the door to his future.... This was the door that would lead from failure to success, *and he couldn't open it!*

The psychiatrist thought for a moment, then asked the man, "You have this dream every time you sleep?"

The man nodded yes.

The doctor said, "Tonight, before you close your eyes, I want you to give yourself the suggestion that when you come to the door again, you're going to notice everything about it, every detail no matter how insignificant you think it is. Then come back tomorrow and tell me what you've seen."

When the doctor saw the man the next day, he couldn't believe his eyes! Gone was the shaken, shrunken fellow who was there the day before. This man looked vibrant and alive. His eyes were bright and he was smiling! The doctor quickly ushered the man into his office for an explanation.

The psychiatrist asked what had happened and the man explained.

"I went to sleep like you told me to, and I gave myself the suggestion to notice and remember every detail about the door to success – so I did. When I came up to the door, I pushed harder than I ever had before. I strained against it – pushing and pushing. Finally, I stood back and looked at the door. And you know what I saw?"

"No," said the doctor, excitedly. "Tell me, tell me."

The man smiled and said, "There was a sign on the door. It said, 'PULL'."

Are You Pushing against the Door to Success?

Are you straining to get ahead in life, struggling against the odds, pushing to get ahead only to find yourself locked out – stuck in a dead-end rut with no way out?

Well, quit pushing!

Pull.

The door to the future – the door to the American Dream – is wide open for you. There's no struggle involved... no nightmare of fear.... All you have to do is what the Bible tells you:

"Ask, and it shall be given you; seek and you shall find; knock, and it shall be opened unto you."

That is, *if* it's the door to Network Marketing.

As you've seen throughout this book – and more importantly, in your own experience – all doors do *not* lead to the future you desire.

Network Marketing can and does.

Millions of people just like you and me have passed through Network Marketing's door to a richer, more rewarding life. They've learned from direct experience how they can have their cake and eat it, too.

Today these people own a business of their own. They're the boss, the CEO of their own growing enterprise – working when they choose, where they choose, with whom they choose.

Network Marketers choose whether they work part-time or full-time, and many who began just to supplement their incomes have made Network Marketing their full-time career.

Network Marketers have learned the power of leverage, what J. Paul Getty meant when he said, "I'd rather have one percent of 100 peoples' efforts than

100 percent of my own." They've seen how a lot of people doing a little bit each can keep all the qualities of "small is beautiful," and yet, accomplish a big, BIG job.

They've experienced – or begun to experience – going beyond mere security to true financial freedom: having all the money they need . . . doing what they want when, they want . . . with no one to tell them otherwise.

You know, 80 percent of all bankruptcies would be prevented if people had as little as an extra $500 per month! In Network Marketing thousands and thousands of people have that – and thousands more have 10, 20, 100 times that – and more!

"I Can't See Myself in Network Marketing"

People tell me that all the time.

"I'm a doctor"... I'm a lawyer... a printer... a teacher"... whatever. I can't see myself in Network Marketing.

When they tell me that, here's what I say:

"That's interesting. You see, I was going to offer you an opportunity with one of my companies driving a garbage truck. Would you be interested in the job?"

And the answer always is, "Are you nuts!?! I don't want to drive a garbage truck!"

Then I respond with, "I've got another company with an opening that pays a million dollars a year! You'd be perfect for the position. Are you interested in that opportunity?"

They answer, "Absolutely! What do I have to do?"

And I tell them, "It's driving a garbage truck."

One guy summed it all up when he said, "Oh, that's different. That's business."

Well, Network Marketing is different, too. It's business. And it's not the garbage truck business, either. It's BIG business. And you can either make up your mind right now that you won't have anything to do with it – or, you can open up your mind and take advantage of an industry whose time has come.

I mean, what if it actually did provide you with the perfect vehicle for getting all you want out of life?

Can you afford to pass up that possibility?

Taking a Chance on Change

You know, sometimes change is a difficult thing to accept. I know. When I was building boats for $5.50 an hour or waiting on tables for $150 a week, I agonized for months about whether or not I should quit my job – a job I absolutely hated! – and risk getting out of my comfort zone by trying something different.

President John Kennedy once said:

"Change is the law of life. And those who look only to the past or the present are certain to miss the future."

He couldn't have been more right!

Just think: ten years ago, there were no video stores... Five years ago, real estate was booming and the banks were healthy... Just one year ago, there was a Soviet Union...!

The lesson is clear: *change – or get left behind.*

Ask Yourself These Questions:

- Am I truly happy with my current job?

- Am I making all the money I deserve?

- Do I have the time I want for my family . . . for my . . . friends . . . for myself?

- Am I growing and developing personally, at the level I want?

- Am I in control of my own work – my life. . or is someone or something pulling my strings?

- Am I willing to do what it takes to have The American Dream?

Four short years ago I asked myself these same questions – and I didn't like the answers *at all!*

So, I changed. I opened up... took a look... and took the biggest step of my life! I quit pushing and PULLED!

I challenge you to do the same.

I challenge you to ask yourself the toughest questions of all. And if you don't like your answers – like I didn't like mine – then do what I did. Take advantage of Network Marketing now before it's too late.

Why Now Is the Best Time to Get Involved

We've all heard the expression, "Timing is everything in life and business." The key to running a successful business ... or to getting rich ... is to get in at the right time ... to get in on a business explosion just before the boom ... to catch a wave just as it starts to rise.

There are four phases of growth in the cycle of any successful business or industry. First is the **Foundation Phase**. Next, the **Concentration Phase**. Then comes the **Momentum Phase**. And last, the **Stability Phase**.

You could call the Foundation Phase the pioneering years. The business is just getting started, and the general public doesn't understand what you're doing because it's "new" and "unproven." The pioneering years are tough. Lots of rejection . . . lots of ups and downs while the foundation is being laid. These are the high risk years.

It's like the pioneers who settled the West. Because they were the first ones to open up the frontier, they had the first shot at the best land. But they were also the ones who got the arrows in their backs!

The Foundation Phase for Network Marketing started in the late 1940's and lasted until 1979, when Amway won a landmark court decision against the FTC. This decision made it clear – once and for all – that Network Marketing was a legal, legitimate system for selling products and services.

After the pioneering years come the Concentration years. This is when business starts to shift gears, to gain some acceptance from the masses. When the first McDonalds Restaurant opened up, for example, it was little more than a local curiosity. No one but the founder, Roy Kroc, believed it was the beginning of an American institution. By the time the 100th McDonalds opened up, however, this trend-setting franchise was not only gaining acceptance . . . it was generating lots of excitement.

Critical Mass: Headed for Take-off!

Today Network Marketing is at the final stage of the Concentration years . . . and entering the explosive Momentum years! The entire industry is just about to undergo a dynamic phenomenon call **Critical Mass**. When an industry hits Critical Mass, something magical happens. It's like someone pushes a cultural button, and "viola" . . . everybody wants what you've got. Critical Mass means the products have gained popular acceptance, and they become market driven. When Critical Mass hits, growth goes into overdrive . . . and sales begin to explode!

Think about this: In the 60's personal computers didn't even exist. In the 70's, only "techies" owned them. But by the mid 80's, the industry hit Critical Mass . . . and today almost half the homes in North America own a personal computer! The same happened to microwaves. And VCR's. Once they hit Critical Mass -- BOOM . . . sales go through the roof!

Get in . . . and Buckle Up!

The entire Network Marketing industry is just starting to enter Critical Mass . . . which means the next five to six years will be a period of tremendous growth . . . of tremendous opportunity . . . and of tremendous profits!

Folks, mark my works . . . you've got until 1997 to get involved . . . to build your business . . . and to hunker down and hold on until the storm passes! Right now it's projected that only two percent of the population is involved in Networking. But I predict that in the next four to six years, that figure will jump to 10 percent! Which means the vast majority of the money to be made in this industry will likely be made this decade!

You couldn't pick a better time to get involved! In the next few years, average people just like you – perhaps someone in your neighborhood or someone you see at church each Sunday – will make a ton of money in Network Marketing by taking advantage of Critical Mass.

Never before in history have so many people been in a position to take advantage of such an explosive mega-trend. That's what makes Network Marketing so exciting . . . and fantastic! When Network Marketing reaches Critical Mass and explodes all over the world, more people – more average men and women – will grab a piece of the money pie than any movement or opportunity in the history of the world!

The risk is small. The reward is great. And there will never, ever be a better time to get involved than right now!

Do what I did . . . take a chance on an industry whose time has come . . . take a chance on yourself. I dare you to be rich!

■ ■ ■

NOTES

<u>NOTES</u>

NOTES

NOTES